SANDPAPERS

S A N D P A P E R S

The lives and letters
of
Eugene Manlove Rhodes
and
Charles Fletcher Lummis

by Frank M. Clark

Foreword by Keith Lummis

SUNSTONE
PRESS

SANTA FE
NEW MEXICO

First Edition

Printed in the United States of America

10 9 8 7 6 5 4 3 2 1

Library of Congress Cataloging in Publication Data:
Clark, Frank M., 1924-
    Sandpapers: the lives and letters of Eugene Manlove Rhodes and Charles Fletcher Lummis / by Frank M. Clark: foreword by Keith Lummis.
        P.   cm.
    Includes index.
        ISBN 0-86534-211-3 : $14.95
        1. Rhodes, Eugene Manlove, 1869-1934. 2. Lummis, Charlezs Fletcher, 1859-1928. 3. Authors, American-20th century—Biography. 4. Authors, American—19th century—Biography. 5. Authors, American— West (U.S.)—Biography. 6. Editors—United States—Biography. 7. West (U.S.)—Intellectual life. I. Title.
PS3535.H68Z58   1994
818'.409—dc20
[B]   93-33738
                                                            CIP

Published by   Sunstone Press
                 Post Office Box 2321
                 Santa Fe, NM 87504-2321 / USA
                 (505) 988-4418 *orders only* (800) 243-5644
                 FAX (505) 988-1025

TABLE OF CONTENTS

Preface / 7
Foreword / 9
Con Apreciacion / 11

Part One
EUGENE MANLOVE RHODES, WESTERN CHRONICLER
Chapter One
The Forming Years: The Setting, The Man / 13
Chapter Two
With Pen in Hand / 24
Chapter Three
Rangeland Romances? / 30
Chapter Four
Domesticity, New Mexico Style / 42
Chapter Five
Apalachin Confinement / 49
Chapter Six
Lost in Los Angeles / 55
Chapter Seven
Trek to the Final Exile / 62
Chapter Eight
By the Shores of the Sundown Sea / 80

Part Two
CHARLES FLETCHER LUMMIS, WESTERN EDITOR
Chapter Nine
The Arrival / 87
Chapter Ten
Birth of a Stormy Petrel / 89

Chapter Eleven
Lummis the Printer / *93*
Chapter Twelve
The Trek / *96*
Chapter Thirteen
City Editor—and Scout / *99*
Chapter Fourteen
New Mexico Interlude / *102*
Chapter Fifteen
At the Editor's Desk Again / *109*
Chapter Sixteen
El Alisal: The Magnificent Dream / *112*
Chapter Seventeen
The Southwest Museum / *117*
Chapter Eighteen
"Always Your Friend" Letters from Lummis / *121*
Chapter Nineteen
The Sunset Years / *130*
Chapter Twenty
Wherein, We Conclude / *145*

A Tribute to Keith Lummis / 151
Bibliography / 153
Index / 154
About the Author / 159

PREFACE

On a sunny warm spring morning ten years ago, I sat on the late W. H. Hutchinson's patio sipping his coffee and bending his ear on my favorite topic, Eugene Manlove Rhodes. Hutch was, as usual, the soul of patience as he listened to my ramblings. He'd heard it all before. When I expressed my great desire to examine the materials he had donated to the Henry E. Huntington Library in San Marino; material he had gathered during his research for his biography of Rhodes, *A Bar Cross Man*, he perked up and growled, "Why don't you go down and look at them. Tell them you want to write a book on Gene from a different slant."

When our visit was at an end, I thanked Hutch for taking the time to see me. He allowed, with a perfectly straight face, that he felt it was his Christian duty.

Getting into the archives at Huntington Library was not that simple. It took a letter from Hutch and one from another friend who was a published writer to convince them of my sincerity, and a few long distance phone calls before I was allowed past the guards and ushered into a large hushed room.

There I was presented with six dusty green boxes tied with twine. To me it was like Christmas. I opened each one eagerly to go through time faded letters, newspaper clippings, old photographs and Hutch's notes he'd written thirty years earlier.

Sitting there going through Hutch's files, I resolved, really for the first time, that I *would* write about Gene Rhodes. I took notes for a week, thanked the librarian, and came home to take ten years to do what I should have been able to do in ten months. In the years that followed I made three more trips to Huntington Library to gain more information.

The many interruptions that plagued me created a sincere sympathy for Gene's distractibility.

A few years, and several visits with Hutch later, he mentioned that Charles Fletcher Lummis' son, Keith Lummis, lived in San Francisco and might be willing to talk to me about Gene and his connection with Lummis. By that time I was becoming more aware of Charles Lummis' influence on Gene and his writing. And so it came about that one morning I took courage and called Keith Lummis' number. A rumbling but not unkind voice answered. After a stammered self introduction, I invited myself to come and talk to him about Gene and his father. To my surprise he was perfectly agreeable. We set a time and date and a few days later I found myself knocking on a door at the top of a long flight of stairs. I was admitted into the home of Keith Lummis and his lovely wife, Hazel.

I sat on the edge of the couch in their living room for two hours and listened spellbound while Keith talked about his famous father, his sister Turbesé and the book that he and Turbesé had started, and he had finished following her death. He willingly shared with me letters that Gene had written to Turbesé while he was an exile in Los Angeles, which gave me a rare insight into an important part of Gene's life.

By this time I was becoming torn between the desire to write about Gene Rhodes and to write about Charles Lummis.

The summer following my first visit with Keith, I went back to Southern California to spend research time in the Braun Library at the Southwest Museum. There I went through the extensive file of Lummis' correspondences with Gene Rhodes, Mary Austin, Maynard Dixon and other artists to whom Charles had written. I found such a strong link between Eugene Manlove Rhodes and Charles Fletcher Lummis in their correspondence that I decided to write of both, including enough of their correspondence to allow the reader to experience for himself the warm bond of friendship that existed between these two noble Southwesterners.

—*Frank M. Clark* *Tehama, California*

FOREWORD

Two good men, Lummis and Rhodes. They loved a good fight as much as a good laugh and they gave their strength to support their friends and confound their enemies. In each was a shred of the chivalric knight questing the modern equivalent of the dragon. Both were armed with pen and fist. Lummis favored the former, Rhodes, the latter. Both adored the fair maiden, one from afar, the other more intimately.

One difference was that Gene Rhodes could invent a plot, create characters for it and pull the necessary strings for them to carry it out. Charles F. Lummis could not do this. He knew it and was unhappy about it. He knew Gene could and admired him for it.

Their similar temperaments developed in quite different backgrounds. Lummis, the preacher's son, was born into a scholarly and ecclesiastical atmosphere. Rhodes grew up on the frontier and only through his mother's reading was he introduced to the world of literature. Yet both had similar loves—books, the rough life of the frontier and the frontier mores. While Gene was breaking horses for $25 a month, Charlie cut out a horse from a herd of mustangs and broke it for his own riding. Instinctively they had the same enemies; falsehood, pretense, arrogance, tyranny. They lent their support to those they felt unjustly accused or abused. Among the many that Lummis unhorsed with his trusty pen were a professor of an eastern university, a clergyman and the Century Dictionary. Gene used the same potent weapon in defense of a long dead Spanish pioneer, a valiant contemporary lawman and he joined Joaquin Miller and Mary Austin in a series of poems published in Lummis' *Land of Sunshine* excoriating the British Empire for its attack on the Afrikaner.

Perhaps if he (Gene) had read less of romantics like Rostand and a bit more of Cervantes he would not have felt impelled to make fistic attack on one of the aggressive Empire's minions who was in Texas buying horses for use in the conquest of South Africa. But perhaps he would have, anyway. He was touchy on that subject.

This book is about interesting people and is worth reading.

—*Keith Lummis*

Editors note: Biography of Keith Lummis appears on page 150.

CON APRECIACION

I want to express a deep and sincere feeling of appreciation to Keith and Hazel Lummis for their hospitality and assistance. I also wish to thank the Henry E. Huntington Library and the Braun Research Library, Southwest Museum, for their assistance and cooperation.

A word of thanks goes to all my friends who helped; especially Patricia Wellingham Jones, who willingly gave of her talents and patience, to the cause.

Most importantly, I want to thank my loving wife, Mildred, for her patience, faith and forbearance during the times when she was a "word processor widow" as I plugged away trying to finish the job.

I wish to dedicate this effort to the memory of the late William Henry Hutchinson, a gentle man as ever was.

Eugene Manlove Rhodes, age 74:
taken two weeks prior to his
death in June, 1934.

PART ONE

EUGENE MANLOVE RHODES, 1869 - 1934
Chronicler of the Southwest

The Setting

New Mexico is as much a state of mind as it is a state of the Union. To the enchantable it truly is a "Land of Enchantment". To the prosaic it offers nothing but wind, dust, heat and bitter winter chills. It is as different from its sister state, Arizona, as California is different from Oregon. Its appeal is similar to the appeal of horseradish or bagpipe music. You either hate it or love it. There's no "sort of" about it.

New Mexico offers wide open expanses framed by majestic snow covered mountains, strangely beautiful rock formations, clear mountain streams and desert rivers that sink from sight. You can leave dry dusty Albuquerque and, in a matter of minutes, be in knee deep snow among tall pines in the Sandia Range.

In probably no other state is history so much a part of daily life. Remnants of New Mexico's violent and turbulent past are on every hand. Towns like Lincoln, Tularosa and Santa Fe appear much the same as they did a hundred years ago, except for the power lines strung overhead, and the paving underfoot. You can almost hear and expect to see, the mountain men, Indians and Spanish soldiers in the plaza in front of the Governor's Palace at Santa Fe. The blending of American, Pueblo Indian and Mexican cultures, in the last 175 years, has resulted in a rich, colorful and extremely inviting life style. The Pueblo Indians remain as mysterious and remote a society as ever, but their haunting architecture is copied over and over by Anglos who are so spellbound by it.

New Mexico today is still largely unoccupied as you will learn should you experience car trouble far from the city. In the 1880's, it was almost as geographically isolated as the moon's surface. Though crossed by rail lines in 1883, New Mexico was devoid of any roads save wagon tracks and horse trails. Citizens had to be self sufficient and innovative to survive. Trips to the store sometimes occurred only once or twice a year. Diet was confined usually to biscuits, beans and beef (sometimes from another man's herd) garnished with chilies and what vegetables the ranch wife was able to grow in a garden she didn't have time to tend. In that time, New Mexico was, as someone said, "Great for men, horses and dogs, but hell on women and kids".

Chapter 1

The Forming Years

At noon on a hot dusty day in 1883, three sixteen year old boys stood on the windswept shoulder of a Southern New Mexico mountain admiring their handiwork. They were nearly men; wiry lads with stringy muscles and calloused hands. Their dirty faces reflected a combination of weariness and satisfaction. As they packed their tools and tightened cinches, they viewed with a great deal of pride the product of their joint efforts, a simple native stone cabin.

Hired by Pres Lewis, the rancher upon whose homestead they stood, the three, in a week's labor punctuated by high jinks and hilarity, had built a house. Crude and rough though it was, it would stand for many years to shelter its owner from icy blasts of winter and the hot winds of summer. Its ruins can still be seen on Animas Creek, northeast of Hillsboro.

Having made their last joke, flung their last jibe, their laughter fading in the wind, the three shook hands, climbed on their horses and moved away. Two headed west. They were soon out of sight. The third, after a last long look at the cabin, headed his horse eastward, toward Engle, and home.

The next day the two westbound boys were ambushed by a band of Geronimo's Apache reservation jumpers and brutally slain. One died with his own crowbar driven through his head.

The eastbound boy was destined to become one of the Southwest's most skilled storytellers. His name was Eugene Manlove Rhodes.

It is an interesting comment on rural American nineteenth century society that three sixteen-year-old boys would be entrusted to build a permanent dwelling, be it ever so humble. At a time when family survival meant dawn-to-dusk labor for all, boys became men long before whiskers appeared. Gene Rhodes, already an accomplished well digger at thirteen, stonemason and roadbuilder at sixteen, was a prime source of income for the Rhodes family. In his middle teens, Gene also worked as a swamper for a freight rig, caring for the horses, their harness and the rolling stock. He served for eighteen months as a civilian guide for the cavalry out of Fort Stanton in its vain efforts to capture ancient Nana, one of the last Apache war chiefs to terrorize ranchers in the early 1880's.

Eugene Manlove Rhodes

Gene Rhodes, born on a dry farm in Nebraska in 1869, came to New Mexico with his parents in 1881. That was the year Pat Garrett took the life of Billy the Kid, three years after the McSween-Murphy feud was ended in Lincoln. Lew Wallace, author of *BEN HUR*, sat in the territorial governor's chair in Santa Fe.

Gene took to the hard life in New Mexico like a kitten takes to cream. A slender handsome youth of somewhat less than average size and suffering from a speech handicap, (he never could pronounce "Rhodes" distinctly) he made up in sheer grit, determination and a monumental wit for his physical shortcomings. Although small in stature, he never lacked the important ingredient, courage. If the occasion warranted it, and it often did in the days of his youth, Gene would fight with joy in his heart and a gleam in his eye. That is not to say he never lost a fight. He lost many of them. But if he was able, he always bounced back with a grin, ready for more. Many of the men Gene fought gave up in disgust because he wouldn't stay down.

In his declining years, Gene once confessed to a friend that he had been involved in 65 fist fights during his lifetime.

Gene's father, Colonel Hinman Rhodes, distinguished himself on the battlefield with honor and great courage during the Civil War but seemed destined to fail at every peacetime business venture he undertook. He tried dry farming; crops failed. He tried selling sewing machines door-to-door on the hot dusty roads of southeastern Kansas. He combined a prodigious capacity for sustaining physical effort and a keen intellect but seemed to lack commercial shrewdness. Unsuccessful in his attempts to provide for his family, he evidently followed someone's well meaning advice and moved to New Mexico. He homesteaded a ranch near the town of Engle, at that time a bustling railroad and cattle shipping center in south central New Mexico. Engle has long since disappeared but it was the center of Gene's world for a number of years. Colonel Rhodes worked as a miner, often developing the claims of others.

Gene spent a great deal of time in his early teens working with his father. He acquired considerable skill in mining, stonemasonry, drilling and use of explosives. His well digging ability became much in demand in the area around Engle. He was once called upon to clear out a one-hundred-sixty-five foot well whose walls had partially collapsed. In addition he was the builder of the first road from Engle to Tularosa, over the San Andres mountains, punching through a pass that bore his name, Rhodes' Pass. This road is no longer to be found on any map since much of it crossed the White Sands Proving Grounds and was later closed to the public.

At sixteen Gene found his first love, horse wrangling. He gave up his masonry work and well drilling to become a top-of-the-line horseman. He quickly became a man who could do anything with a horse. He not only rode and broke any bronc from the sorriest scrub to the wildest range stallion at hand, but he made it seem so easy. He almost became a legend in his own time. His employment on local ranches, including the Bar Cross Ranch, came about because of his skill with horses. He was never a skilled cowman.

At nineteen, in 1888, Gene's skills and general knowledge acquired through extensive reading, enabled him to gain entrance into what is now called College of the Pacific, located in Stockton, California. At that time it was known as The University of the Pacific, and was located at San Jose, California.

Why Gene selected this, a Methodist school, so far from his beloved New Mexico, is not known. It is known, however, that his mother was a staunch Methodist. At any rate, it provided Gene with some much needed socializing experiences and was the one time in his younger days when he could be and act young. It was, in his own words,"...the happiest of my life. Not one care, not one unhappy moment...I had never known any boys. Just rough men. I had my youth in one deep, priceless draught."

Gene had been forced by financial circumstances into manhood at thirteen, had done a man's work since that time. This then was his one chance to be a boy for a time. He engaged in athletic events, he joined the Rhyzomian Literary Society and was among the list of officers the second year as "critic." His first published works, unsigned, appeared in the college newspaper.

During the summer of 1889, Gene joined harvest crews and roamed the Salinas Valley from Salinas to King City working on the threshing rigs as the wheat crop ripened in the hot California sunshine.

Rhodes family tradition has it that Gene borrowed $50.00 from his father to get himself to California and enrolled. The rest of his expenses for two years, he earned himself.

One close friend he made at college was indirectly to have a profound impact on Gene's future. His name was Sydney Martin Chynoweth. He graduated from University of the Pacific in 1890, the same year Gene returned to New Mexico. He either accompanied Gene home, or followed him soon after. He went to work the following fall as teacher of the one room school at Alto in Lincoln County.

Gene's father was then Agent for the Mescalero Apache Reservation and he appointed Gene as Reservation Farmer, a decision he was later to regret when a political faction from Santa Fe, the notorious "Santa Fe Ring," worked to get him removed. One of the charges made against him was nepotism.

On a dark night in early February, 1891, Gene and a friend, on their way home from an evening social function, were attacked by a Doña Ana County deputy sheriff and a seven man posse. This group did not identify itself, but called out for the boys to stop from the shadows of the cottonwoods that lined the street. Gene responded by jumping into the middle of the posse, fists flying. He was nearly killed. A doctor friend later counted thirteen head wounds from pistol whipping. A bullet fired at him traveled across his skull under his scalp.

The Rio Grande Republican, a newspaper owned by a member of the Santa Fe Ring, reported that Gene was "furiously drunk". Colonel Rhodes contended that the incident was purely an effort to put him in disrepute with the Department of Indian Affairs.

Gene was charged with "Resisting an Officer," and "Drawing a Deadly Weapon" The case was moved to Sierra County and the charges were dismissed.

In February, 1891, Gene was released as Reservation Farmer and Syd Chynoweth was confirmed in his place. In April 1891 Gene took over Syd's job as teacher and completed the school year. He was not rehired, but went back to wrangling horses for local ranchers.

Eventually he wound up working for the Bar Cross Ranch, herding horses and working cattle. By common consensus, including his own, Gene was never a top line cowman. He carried his weight, but his heart wasn't in it. He went with what he knew, and liked, and that was horses, reading, and poker. He homesteaded 80 acres around a spring in the San Andres mountains, built a rough cabin and corrals and leased it to Bar Cross for a horse watering camp. The money from this transaction went, as did most of the money he made, to his parents. Later, he tried horse ranching, trapping wild horses and rough breaking them to sell when you could hardly even give a good horse away. Which brings us to an episode in Gene's life that demonstrates a facet of his personality, and which he later used as the basis for a story, (Loved I Not Honor More), his sixth published piece of fiction.

Word came to Gene, at a time when he seemed to owe everyone money, that a buyer was paying top money ($25.00) for rough broken mounts in El Paso, Texas. All Gene had was lots of horses. He saw a chance to move some stock and get some creditors off his neck at the same time, which he badly needed to do. He forthwith rounded up the best of his herd and lit a shuck for El Paso.

When he arrived, Gene was dumbfounded to learn that the buyer was an English army officer purchasing mounts for the British cavalry to take to South Africa to fight the Boers. Now Gene wouldn't have known a Boer from a Zulu, but he knew about underdogs, and from what he'd read about the Boer War, he knew it wasn't a fair fight. The British Empire was putting all its strength, and that of its allies, against a small group of people that seemed only to want to be left alone. Gene was not about to aid and abet the effort. He rounded up his herd and headed home, but not before he had insulted the Briton and egged him into fisticuffs. The captain won, narrowly, but Gene, having struck several blows for the underdog, went home in clouds of dust and righteousness, knowing that solvency had once again evaded his clutches.

(Loved I Not Honor More) appeared in the February 1903 issue of *Out West* magazine. It was essentially a fictionalized version of Gene's El Paso trip. The foundation for the story was Gene's philosophy; master of no man, servant of none. This was the major theme of everything he ever wrote.

Back at the ranch, not only was Gene sorely pressed for cash, but he was also seriously contemplating matrimony. It would have been easy to have sold those horses in El Paso and brought home a nest egg. No one would have known or cared about his feelings toward the Boer War, but Gene knew, and while his purse was empty, his conscience was clear.

Gene was never a stranger to poverty. It hampered his movements and plagued his life right to the end. He was, however, the embodiment of Polonius' advice; "To thine own self be true."

Although he was always ready for a scrap, Gene's attitude toward the Boer War pretty much represented his feelings toward all wars. His sympathies went directly to the weaker side regardless of the cause. When the United States won the Spanish American War and assumed sovereignty over the Philippines, he saw it merely as an exchange of overlords, a trade of a velvet collar for an iron one. Both hampered individual freedom in Gene's eyes, and made the citizens of the Philippines second class citizens.

Such behavior typified Gene's quixotic and chivalric character. Inherently compassionate, gentle and kind to those smaller or weaker than himself, he never hesitated to fight for those causes he deemed worthy of his defense, against any odds of any size. An honorable and gallant warrior himself, he readily

recognized honor and gallantry in others, be it every so minus-
cule.

   In an early letter to Charles Lummis he wrote this about the
final, bloody battle of the Lincoln County War, when the McSween
home was burned to the ground to drive out its defenders.

   —concentrating on one twelve seconds—briefly—when
McSween's house burned at Lincoln, Billy the Kid's bunch
ran the gauntlet. 10 men—four killed, one left for dead in
twelve seconds.—you know the story... Eight of them ran
at their best zig-zag sweat. McSwain walked to his death.
But O'Folliard stopped in that hell—in the full glare of the
flames—and picked up the body of his friend Harvey
Morris--found him dead, laid the body down—didn't drop it
but laid it down—and so went on his way. I think David's
eyes were wet, and Saxon Harold's hand rose up to greet the
brave.

   Nor was this all. I violate no confidence when I say
that the sixty men whose rifles swept that firelit space were
not saints. Some of them were the lowest of the low. The
best were nothing to write home about. I know some of
these men, and everyone is my enemy. But no bullet struck
Tom O'Folliard—the only man who stood still and offered
a mark impossible to miss—sixty men drunk with hate and
triumph. (Including Bob Beckwith who died ten seconds
later.) Men said in their sixty black hearts, "Somebody else,
not me." Through the smoke and dust and hate, this
generous deed shines like a star. For all that, may all their
sins, which are as scarlet, be forgiven them.

   While the Lincoln County War, which lasted three years and
assured the immortal notoriety of that dull-witted thug, Billy the

Kid, occurred three years before Gene came to New Mexico, Lincoln was right in the middle of Gene's adopted territory. He had ample opportunity to know the denizens of Lincoln County on both sides of the law. Some of the survivors of the final battle at McSween's house were still active at their various pursuits. Tom O'Folliard, horse thief and cattle rustler, had been killed by Pat Garrett at Fort Sumner, but Gene greatly respected his selflessness, loyalty and bravery under fire.

Chapter 2

"With Pen in Hand"

Gene was educated primarily at his mother's knee. Mrs. Rhodes, well educated for the time, and with a wealth of knowledge about, and a deep love for, literature, instilled that love in Gene at an early age. A handsome, intelligent woman, she was to remain a dominant figure in her son's life.

With the family's many moves and the scarcity of schools in the Midwest of the 1870's, Gene's class time was extremely limited. He quickly displayed, however, an insatiable thirst for learning. As his reading skills progressed, so did his drive to read more and more. He read everything he could get his hands on from tomato can labels to the family Bible. His reading progress was hampered somewhat by a self-inflicted eye wound. At age four, on the Nebraska farm, he had watched a hired man take out a glass eye, wash it and put it back. Gene caused permanent damage to his own eye trying earnestly to do likewise.

Gene had a remarkable talent for retaining much of what he had read and was able to quote whole passages long after he had read them. He also had the ability to become totally engrossed in what he was reading, to the point of forgetting time and place. One New Mexican acquaintance of Gene's youth told of Gene riding up to the front gate, nose in a book, remaining on the horse until he had finished the book, whereupon he climbed down and proceeded with his visit. Another told of Gene being sent to bring in a herd of horses by the foreman and showing up at headquarters, reading a book, but without the horses.

The transition from avid and eclectic reader to writer was a natural one. To one so taken with the power of the printed word, the urge to put his own thoughts down on paper followed as a to-be-expected consequence. His first efforts were an attempt to express poetically, his passion for the New Mexico desert.

Gene's first published piece, signed, was a poem printed in the *Land of Sunshine* magazine in April, 1896. It was entitled "Charlie Graham," and was the story of a dying miner. The editor who published it was Charles Fletcher Lummis, another man of literature whose soul resided in the Southwest desert. Lummis was to become Gene's editor, critic and close friend from 1896 until Lummis' death in 1928. Gene had much to learn and Lummis, seeing the great talent hidden in Gene's sophomoric beginnings, was willing to teach. Lummis was an editor of great skill and he could be merciless with those whose works were of mediocre quality. He would accept nothing but what be considered a writer's best efforts. In Gene Rhodes he had a willing and eager protege.

Gene's mastery of the English language, largely self taught, was nothing short of brilliant. He used words with the precision of surgical instruments. His own grammatical usage was flawless. When he began to write fiction, shortly before he married, his characters also spoke the King's English correctly. Never a "Ah seen 'im" or "you-all" or the so-called western drawl we have come to associate with "westerns". He left all that to Owen Wister, Zane Grey, Bower, Seltzer and the other purveyors of "blood and thunder" pulp fiction. The men he wrote about, he knew. They didn't talk that way.

Gene was a born writer. He was never a willing one. He once said, "if there was anything else I could do to make a living, nothing would induce me to touch a pen or pencil again."

At a time when popular writers were cranking out one book after another, Gene's total production was seven. Of these, most started existence as novellas, padded to fill a publisher's concept of how many pages a two-dollar book should have. This effort represented thirty years of his life.

Two personality flaws prevented more volume. One was his eagerness to be distracted from the writing task at hand. If visitors dropped by, often to Mrs. Rhodes' distress; if a baseball game was imminent; if another author's book caught his eye; all work was laid aside until the distraction was dealt with. He once went four and a half years without publishing a single word.

The other flaw was a relentless perfectionism. For every word of every Rhodes story published, Gene probably wrote ten. He was constantly re-writing, adding, deleting, searching for a better way to express his ideas. On at least one occasion, and there were undoubtedly more, he spent a whole day pacing his study trying to come up with the one word he needed to complete a phrase. Gene's writing may have been a labor of love. It was always labor.

And then there was the matter of a failing body and a damaged heart that could not keep up with his ever seeking mind, that could not provide the physical energy needed to keep up with the demands publishers put upon him. After his poor health had exiled him to Pacific Beach in Southern California, there were times when the walk from the house to his studio in the back yard left him too exhausted to work.

Whether or not his ailments were a result of breathing rock dust in his well digging days, Gene was plagued with asthma and influenza all his adult life. An early siege damaged his heart, seriously hampering his physical well-being and, ultimately, forcing an exile from his beloved New Mexico. The dust and winds were too much for his weakened respiratory system. This internal struggle between the body's weakness and the mind's drive produced a tendency toward melancholy and hypochondria. His constantly dwindling income contributed greatly. The death of his 20 month-old-daughter in 1910 nearly robbed him of the will to live.

In spite of his physical ills, writer's blocks, and demands made upon his time by publishers, relatives, friends and struggling young writers, Gene remained patient, witty, kind and gentle to all who approached him, to the end. At the same time his soul harbored much bitterness.

Gene felt his publishers were not giving his books the publicity they deserved. To the publishers of the day, Gene's books were "westerns." It deeply offended Gene to see his works compared to and sold with books by Zane Grey, Clarence E. Mulford and Charles Alden Seltzer, writers whose works were, in Gene's own words, "Every book false on every page in letter and in spirit—sour grapes don't express it. I could have bitten a twenty penny nail in two."

To Gene Rhodes and his band of fans and supporters, and to other knowledgeable writers, such as J. Frank Dobie, Bernard DeVoto and Walter Prescott Webb, who knew the real west, it was like comparing Model T Fords and Packards because they both ran on four wheels.

Gene's publishers, on the other hand, have to be given credit for a certain amount of patience. In 13 years, Houghton Mifflin Publishing Company had received only three books by Gene to publish. *Stepsons of Light* was published June 3, 1921. *Copper Streak Trail* followed with creditable speed, on May 5 1922. The third, *Once in the Saddle,* didn't appear until April 29, 1927. Total sales of these three books had been less than 18,000 copies and only one, *Copper Streak Trail,* made it into Grosset and Dunlap reprints. Gene's next novel, *The Trusty Knaves,* didn't get published until November 1, 1931.

Nothing can keep a writer's works on the public mind or on library shelves with such gaps. Grey, Mulford and Seltzer were turning out that many books per year. In addition, Gene's books were consistently 30 to 60 pages shorter than other "westerns" selling at the standard price of $2.00. Even the staunchest Rhodes fan can understand that Houghton Mifflin was in business to sell books.

Another windmill against which Gene pitted his pen, especially in his later years, with little success and much frustration was the changing American social attitude toward labor, love, sex and patriotism. The particular objects of his wrath were the "Lost Generation" writers: Sinclair Lewis, Ernest Hemingway, William Rose Benet and social critics like H. L. Mencken. These writers had gained attention by deriding American society as cultureless and colorless while praising Europe and its cultural superiority. Rhodes called them the "Euromerican critics of the revolting school." They seemed to deride the very things Gene honored above all else: the unsung valor of the common man and the honor of physical labor.

In a 1925 letter to historian Bernard DeVoto, he wrote, "I find myself in a peculiar position in regards to these people *(Mencken, et al.).* Except for the one item of physical labor, I share their rebellions. I am of no religion: never believed one word of it; and deplore bigotry. I think pleasure desirable and needful. I distrust education as practiced: hate prudery, think that the workings of our courts is a mockery, that New England's social and literary superciliousness is absurd. I hate jingoism, militarism -- and so on for quantity. Yet I have never been able to convince myself that any man is base merely because he did not agree with me upon these subjects. Item: most of my pleasure and interest is derived from the arts—music, poetry and prose — also why not, mountains, nights, days, dawns and seas. Are not these things and art enjoyed at first hand? Or must they be copied? Yet I have never believed that nothing counted but art, that the part is greater than the whole. And as much as I dislike the Puritan snivel, when I look back on life, it seems that if really forced to choose between snivel and sneer, I must prefer the snivel. It seems more manly than the sneer."

Gene energetically scoffed at the modern (of his time) love stories written by so-called realists who "write of love as nothing different from the adventures of an alley cat." In one letter he described the modern love story as simply "an account of how to reduce the swelling of an inflamed penis."

The frontiersman characteristics that Gene held so dear; honesty, personal courage, generosity, manliness, courtesy, especially toward women, were of a time past. The honorable bond of a handshake agreement, the pride in the results of hard physical labor, now appeared to mean little. What was of vital importance to Gene, seemed unimportant and old fashioned in the 1920s and 1930s.

Of H. L. Mencken, Gene once wrote, "The Clan Mencken are no more qualified to write about Americans than I am to write about the engines of the Mauretania. I know nothing about marine engines. Mr. Mencken and his little play-fellows know nothing of the loyalty and valor, strength and wisdom that drive America. All they know is the First Cabin and the upper deck."

Chapter 3

Rangeland Romances?

Gene's stories seldom included members of the gentler sex. His best ones had them not at all. When women appeared, the characterization was invariably less than three dimensional. They were all, as Bernard DeVoto once said, "Infrangibly virginal," which is how the lonely Gene, with the cleft palate, viewed the ranch girls of his youth.

The lovelife of an almost perennially penniless horsewrangler is sparse and seldom, to say the least. Gene Rhodes was no exception. He included many rancher's daughters in his circle of friends, but according to Bob Martin, a close friend and an able cowhand, "Gene liked the girls to chat with and put life into, but no familiarities." Gene wholeheartedly fell in love with only one girl, Miss May Bailey, who visited the Rhodes homestead with her parents while Gene was still in his teens. She became the basis for Gene's fictional heroines ever after. Nothing came of the romance. Mrs. Rhodes and Mrs. Bailey struck sparks off each other and coolness developed between the families. Gene and May went their separate ways. May probably never realized the effect she had had on Gene.

It is fairly certain that Gene was not unacquainted with the fleshpots of El Paso and the surrounding area. He did not write of the women he encountered there.

May Davison Purple

The events that led to the marriage of Eugene Manlove Rhodes and May Louise Purple, nee Davison were circuitous, to say the least. They are as follows:

Colonel Hinman Rhodes served a short time as agent for the Mescalero Apache Reservation. He received the appointment as a result of strong support by the citizens of Socorro County and by endorsement of the *Lincoln County Leader* editor. He did not have the support of New Mexico's ruling politicos in Santa Fe. They were pushing their own man for the position. The reservation was prime grazing land, much misused by cattlemen whose ranches adjoined the reservation and who supported the state politicians. The position of reservation agent was a political plum and a lucrative one, as well.

Colonel Rhodes was too honest to be allowed to stay. He rejected cattle that were too thin. He paid only for what was actually shown as scale weight. He vigorously insisted that agency employees deliver full rations and other allowances to the Apaches. He also committed a grave error in hiring Mrs. Rhodes as reservation matron, and Gene as reservation farmer. The Santa Fe politicians brought charges against Rhodes of, "Incapacity due to age and infirmity of temper." They also brought a charge of nepotism against Rhodes because he hired family members. On April 22, 1892, President Harrison removed Colonel Rhodes from office. No reason was given.

Colonel Rhodes joined Mrs. Rhodes and their daughter, Helen, in Mesilla, New Mexico where Mrs. Rhodes had settled following her removal from the reservation. In 1896 he was turned down for the position of Custodian of Government Property at Fort Stanton, by then abandoned. Clarence, Gene's brother, graduated that summer from the New Mexico State College at Las Cruces and went to Mexico as a mining engineer. He remained there for most of the balance of his life.

Mrs. Rhodes, who quite possibly had grown disenchanted with both New Mexico and the colonel, sold the property in Mesilla and moved to Pasadena, California. Colonel Rhodes "hung around" Gene's ranch and stayed with various friends for two years before he joined Mrs. Rhodes in California.

In the interim, Mrs. Rhodes became re-acquainted with an old family friend, Sidney Chynoweth, and formed close ties with his parents who resided nearby.

At the Chynoweth home Mrs. Rhodes met a trained nurse, Emma Davison, who had known the Chynoweths when they had lived near her parent's home in Apalachin, New York. Mrs. Rhodes and Miss Davison became close friends. In conversation, Miss Davison told Mrs. Rhodes about her baby sister May, back home in New York, and the tragedy that had befallen her.

May's husband, Fred Purple, walking the railroad tracks with his younger brother, Bob, had failed to hear a locomotive coming up from behind. Alerted too late, he managed to save Bob, but fell beneath the massive drivers and was killed. May, widowed, pregnant and with a 16 month old son, Jack, was residing with her parents on their farm. May's parents were becoming increasingly overwhelmed by the rigors of maintaining a rocky farm as their years advanced.

Mrs. Rhodes, in turn, told Miss Davison about her talented son in New Mexico and gave her some of his poems to read. Mrs. Rhodes also took it upon herself to write to Gene and tell him of May's tragedy. Emma Davison returned to Apalachin to nurse May through a severe attack of diphtheria. To entertain her while she recuperated, she read Gene's poems aloud. May was intrigued. The result was a two year non-stop correspondence between Mrs. May Purple and Mr. Eugene Manlove Rhodes which gained in intensity and volume until Gene finally decided to go east and see for himself this lady correspondent who admired his poetry so much.

Broke as usual, and with a ranch full of half-broken horses to feed and water, Gene set about making preparations for the trip east. His lack of the price of a train ticket bothered him not at all. He found a bum wandering through Engle, dirty, lousy and starving. He got the man cleaned up, fed and installed as caretaker of the ranch in his absence. In order that the man, Hargis by name, would have food, Gene shot and slaughtered a young beef not his own. It was, in fact, the property of Tom Catron, one of the ranchers who had helped get Gene's father removed as reservation agent. (Which may have greatly improved the flavor.)

Gene then borrowed $35.00 from his friend Bob Martin, and hopped a freight loaded with cattle bound for the Kansas City slaughterhouses. He was hired as a "shipper" and armed with a cattle prod. At the Kansas City stockyards, Gene met an old friend from the Jornada, Fred Forsha, now in the livestock commission business. Forsha entertained Gene for a few days and got him a ride on a trainload of beeves headed for Liverpool, England via New York City.

On that leg of the journey Gene tangled with an ex-prizefighter member of the train crew. Gene won the fight, but arrived in New York tattered, dirty, with one ear slightly loosened and two black eyes. He laid over in New York long enough to begin healing, and to "See the elephant".

Of his arrival in Apalachin on July 18, 1899, May later wrote, "I heard the faraway train whistle. After sufficient pause, I craned my neck out the little upstairs window as Connie McMahon's shacking team and old canvas-covered stage ambled up the valley road. A solitary passenger stepped out. I scudded down to Spooky Bridge. There, I met him." "Him" was a rather small, wiry man permanently sunburned, with a heavy mustache, strong toil-scarred hands and a pair of blue eyes that seemed "to look right through you". His face appeared a bit battered. He was 30 years old.

Later, she wrote, "We kissed each other, a bit timidly I'll allow, and hand-in-hand, we paced slowly up the hill to the house." In Gene's cheap cardboard suitcase were his gifts to May: a volume of Rudyard Kipling's poems and a pearl-handled pistol.

Courtship was impeded by May's two boys who saw Gene was a new source of entertainment. Gene and May were married on August 9th, 1899. Gene didn't actually make his formal proposal until after the parson had arrived. A few days later, Gene left for New Mexico without his new family because he didn't have train fare for them. It would be interesting to know what went through May's mind as she said goodby to her husband of four days.

Back at the ranch, Gene found himself not only broke but in trouble with the law. Seems his temporary caretaker ate the beef Gene left him, then turned him in for killing it. Catron, at that time, had a standing reward of $500.00 for violators of his property.

Unwisely, the wretched Hargis neglected to leave the country before Gene got back. He had, in fact, taken up residency in White Oaks, where Gene found him. In Gene's own words, "I waylaid Mr. Hargis and induced him to leave the country—escorted him well on his way and rode back to my ranch unobserved." One story has it that Gene bent a pistol barrel over Hargis' head and took him clear to the Texas border with a stern admonition to show his face in New Mexico again only at risk of great peril to himself.

The story also has it that two warrants for Gene's arrest had been issued: one for the already consumed beef, and one for inducing a witness to leave the jurisdiction of the court. Evidently no great effort was made to serve them. Gene's only comment was, "Good men hate traitors—and after what I had done for Hargis, it was bad taste for him to prattle."

During this time, waiting for his new family, Gene began to try his hand at writing fiction, with his usual enthusiasm for new pursuits. Bursting with ideas, and with the patient help of a sympathetic rancher's wife, he began to put together short stories. His first published story, "The Hour and the Man", he sold to Charles Lummis for $10.

He wrote the story in longhand, shipped it to New York where May rented a typewriter and made it legible. It began, "There are three well beaten paths marked out for the feet of young men disappointed in love. The one most commonly used is to marry another girl and forget. Next to this in popularity, is to be studiously reckless and consume large quantities of malt and spiritous liquors; this being generally considered a high tribute to the charms of the lady in the case. Some few remain single and pose as cynics. . . I was one of those who married—and forgot." This story, like all Gene's early ones, was pure frontier Gothic, with only faint glimmerings of the great talent and wit showing through.

Supposedly, Gene had returned to New Mexico to establish a home for May and the boys, but the months flew by and he had little to show for the time spent.

Tularosa N.M. Nov 25 1901.

My dear Summins;

Your letter recd, and will work the Bear over. D.V.

I inclosed two M.SS stories and some verses. They are of the West, wooly. The stories are for your consideration — and as to the the form — can you spare me a quarter of an hour for criticism of it. I know its general faults — that it is too long at one end, and sing-songy because of the recurring last line — could you suggest some particular changes? It is a microscopical account of an actual occurrence with only one additional circumstances interpolated. Every item of the grocery bill and even the proper names are accurate. I would not ask you to do this, were it not notorious that busy people are the only ones who have any leisure to do anything worth while.

Beware of encouraging me on my wild career, lest a worse thing befall you. I am now prepared to furnish stories on the great gross. Regards to Mrs Summins.

Yours truly Eugene M. Rhodes

CHARLIE GRAHAM

Land of Sunshine Magazine--April 1896

From the cliff that frowns beside
Amargosa's bitter tide,
  Charlie Graham's signal light
o'er the desert parched and brown
Flamed its nightly message down,
  "all is well! good night! good night!"

From the shadows, gaunt and gray
Charlie Graham, where he lay
  Dying, by his beacon light
With his last strength and breath
Flashed across the Valley of Death—
  "All is well! good night! good night!"

Where the farthest slopes are dark
One is waiting for the spark
  That should kindle on the height;
Shows her child the sudden star
Where love's message gleams afar--
  "All is well! good night! good night!"

Low she croons a cradle song,
"Sleep, my baby, not for long
  Shall the mine from home delay him."
Sleep, poor mother! dream and rest,
With your babe upon your breast--
  All is well with Charlie Graham!

This was Eugene Manlove Rhodes first published poem. He was paid $10.00.

Engle, N.M. Oct. 7th, 1899

Mr. Chas F. Lummis
Los Angeles Cal.

Dear Sir:
Once I sent you this poem and you returned it with the recommen-
dation to "try again". I have tried again and enclose the result for
your consideration.
Allow me to congratulate you on your manly and fearless stand in
the Philippine Blunder.
Yours-grateful for past favors
Eugene M. Rhodes.

This was one of the first known letters that Gene wrote to
Charles Lummis. It was the beginning of a long and mutually
beneficial correspondence. It was written two months after
Gene's wedding and his return to New Mexico. What poem he is
referring to is not certain. Probably it was "A Ballade of Grey
Hills", first printed by *Land of Sunshine* magazine November
1900. If Lummis, the editor, had not liked the poem he would not
have bothered to return it. Gene was not discouraged by editorial
criticism possibly because he held Lummis' views in such high
regard.

October 18, 1904

Dear Rhodes:
  Why don't you write us a story—or somebody a story? It is a long time since I have seen one of those bully stories of yours.
  What do you say if I take you in hand like a Dutch uncle, pick out the best of your stories, edit them a little further, and submit them myself to the Publishers for a book? Stories, like everything else have to stand on their own bottom; but at least it won't prejudice them if I send along the manuscript. The other day I was looking over three or four of your tales and it struck me again that there is a reasonable chance to get them published in book form although all publishers have a tradition adverse to books of short stories.
  If this should happen to go, it would mean a modest royalty to you and further recognition among those who count. Let me know. Meantime shake your sombrero a little and give us another of those good stories.
    Always
    Your friend
    Chas. F. Lummis

This is a rare early letter to Gene by Lummis. Both were men who wrote frequently and most assuredly had communicated many times before October 1904 when this letter was written, but this was the time when Gene was trying desperately to clean up his indebtedness and save train fare to return to May. Not a well organized person at best, he probably lost most of Lummis' letters traveling around New Mexico, in search of work. A saddlebag makes a poor file cabinet.
  It would surely have been a very encouraging letter to a struggling young writer. Perhaps Gene forwarded it on to May

and she filed it away. It certainly demonstrates the kindness and
warmth Lummis was capable of showing toward those he cared
for.

Tularosa, N. . Mar. 15 (1905)

My dear Lummis
    *Your letter of Mar. 12 enclosing greenback for the Ballade, is
at hand. Check for Ge Ge came before. According to request I
enclose herein M.S.S. Story. I omit the stamps this time.*
    *Please divest yourself of any notion that I light cigarettes with
the checks, or that any apology is needed for the size of them. I
appreciate your position exactly and am sure you pay all you can
afford to at present. I am sure Out West is bound to grow. And
that when it is more prosperous, the checks will be fatter. In the
meantime I am uncommonly glad to get these.*
    *Have two more stories completed which with three others
projected, we intended for a series about the Bar Cross peelers.
But one of them, which chronologically should precede this one,
I am holding back for two reasons. Firstly, because I am not
satisfied with it and secondly because I have a vague feeling that
an incident in it has been used before and want to investigate it.
Will send you the next one in a week or so. There is only one
typewriter in town and I can only get it Sundays. And my mother
has just come to visit me so I don't want to work on it tomorrow.*
    *O, as to the "biography", I never cared much for that kind of
fiction and doubt if the great G.P. (general public) cares much for
this one now. Anyhow, I haven't a halfway decent photo. When
my mother goes back to California, she may bring you her bunch
and let you pick one out.*
    *As to getting a new one, there are three valid objections. First,
there are no photographers in this benighted land, nor even*

kodakers. Secondly, I have been sick and look like the very personal devil. Thirdly, and most important I have no money. So I guess that will have to wait a while. Much obliged to you all the same.

It is told of Cato, the Censor, that, whereas Demetrius Phalerius had 300 statues erected to him by the people of Athens, Cato always evaded such honors on one pretext or another. A friend remonstrated with him whereon he replied that he would rather people would ask why his statue was not there than why it WAS there.

O, by the way—the next story is much better than this one, I think.

Chapter 4

Domesticity: New Mexican Style

Gene hardly seemed ready to assume the role of family man, even at the age of thirty. May not only had the two small boys to raise and care for, but she also felt a deep responsibility toward her aging parents. In the later years of the 19th century, there was little room in American society for a young widowed mother. Women had not yet begun to take their place in the business world except in metropolitan cities. Widows, especially widows with young boys, were pressured to remarry so their sons might have the influence of a father figure to "mold character". The pressure in a stratified tight rural community like Apalachin must have been formidable. Of that small town, Gene later said, "The only traces of democracy on the river road were the school house and the cemetery".

Although May had been trained as a nurse, leaving one's children with a babysitter and going off to work was unthinkable in her time and place. There were few opportunities in rural upstate New York for employment even if May could have found someone willing to take care of the boys. All she really could do was to earn her keep helping her parents and watch for a likely suitor who was willing to take on a readymade family. Gene must have seemed like a gift from heaven to her. Surely, his letters must have convinced her that he was an honorable man who would be kind to her sons. He seemed a man of courage, honor, loyalty and great sincerity. Love would have to come later. It is certain that she had no idea how woefully unprepared to support her and her family Gene actually was.

May didn't arrive in New Mexico for almost a year. No one knows how the train fare was managed. Gene was gambling heavily. Perhaps he won a pot and sent it to her. Perhaps her brother, George Davison, 4 years older than May, and then principal of Gloverville High School in Gloverville, New York, helped out. He was sympathetic to their financial plight and genuinely fond of Gene. He was to be of great help to them and to Gene's writing career in later years.

In June, 1900, May stepped off the train in Tularosa, totally unprepared for the vast difference in the physical environment. The change from the rolling green hills of New York state to the bleak windswept vista of sand and rock must have been a shock to her. She brought with her, her youngest son, Fred. Jack, her oldest, seems to have been left with his grandparents until May could find out about housing. Gene had rented a small house in Tularosa, probably chosen over Engle, which was closer to the ranch, because Tularosa had running water (in a community ditch), trees, gardens and a school for Fred. The teacher was a former student of Gene's, Ula Gilmore.

The house was adobe with a dirt floor. Dust sifted through every crack with every sandstorm and they came with heart-breaking regularity, especially in the spring. May had helpful neighbors, and her accounts of that time sound brave and cheery, but it must have been a lonely and frightening time for the young woman from New York state. Gene was gone most of the time, either trying to make a success of his ranch or gambling with what little proceeds he gained.

Eventually Gene was forced to the realization that he was not living up to his own strict code. That code demanded that a man accept and face up to his responsibilities.

It was a desperate time in a poor land. Gene struggled to mend his ways. He even tried to renew his teaching certificate, thinking he might go back into the classroom. He passed the written examination with ease but was refused the certificate because county officials felt his "moral conduct" was unacceptable. His passion for gambling and his friendship with persons who operated outside the law were well known by his peers on the certification board.

W.H. Hutchinson, in his biography of Gene Rhodes, *A Bar Cross Man,* claimed, "It may be just as well that he did not get a teaching certificate. The small but steady pay of a teacher might have stabilized his life until it was too late for him to do or be aught else." Of a certainty, Gene NEVER completed a book unless he was in dire need of money, and not even then if he were emotionally upset.

On June 12, 1901, May give birth to Alan Hinman Rhodes in the adobe house with the dirt floor. A neighbor acted as midwife. No doctor was ever consulted. Caring for a baby in this alien land, penniless, mostly alone, must have taxed May's resources dreadfully. Her strong sense of humor must have served her well. She didn't get much support from Gene, who seemingly had no more understanding of feminine needs than a bear cub might.

In spite of trying circumstances, a strong bond was building. May was fiercely loyal to Gene and supportive of his writing efforts. He in turn began to depend heavily on her input, her insight and most certainly on her ability to interpret his almost illegible handwriting, and to type his works on a rented typewriter. Her faith and her insistence on consistent effort were paying off. Eight of Gene's stories were purchased by Charles Lummis and published in *Out West.* Probably Lummis, whose budget was always tight, paid $10.00 apiece for them. A momentous occasion during that time was the sale of one story, "His Father's Flag", to *McClure's Magazine* for $40.00. The arrival of that check must have been a joyous occasion for the Rhodes family. May's faith in Gene was beginning to pay off. Even so, May longed for the tranquil green hills of Apalachin.

By late spring of 1902, May had had all she could take. Tired, homesick and ill with almost chronic tonsillitis, she made up her mind to go home. Ostensibly it was to be for a six month visit to give her parents a chance to get acquainted with Alan, and for her to reunite with Jack, her oldest.

Tularosa gossip had it that she had told Gene that if he wanted to see his son again he'd better plan to come to New York. Perhaps she did. It seems more likely that Gene simply couldn't get the money together for their return fare.

May didn't return to New Mexico for twenty-five years. It took Gene four years to accumulate train fare to get him to New York. During the years after May left, Gene sold his horse herd. A flood washed his ranch buildings away, leaving him homeless. He wound up washing dishes, digging wells, swamping out a saloon and working in the Crown Flour Mill in Socorro. One ray of hope was the prospect of a job as editor of the Roswell *Daily Record*. An old friend, Lewis Fort, an ex-newspaper man, worked hard to get Gene this job but the paper's owner was not impressed. Gene's pride was sorely dented by the incident.

Correspondence from the east was not encouraging. May was very ill and Gene was distraught because he could not reach her side. By this time he had been reduced to digging ditches for Oliver Lee to whom he owed $250.00.

In April, 1906, Gene was still working for Oliver Lee on a pipeline across Tularosa Basin. He got involved in a scrap with a two-hundred-fifty pound black man who had cursed him thoroughly. Gene had caught him cheating in a crap game in Orogrande.

Gene was winning by breaking beer bottles over his opponent's head. Someone finally forced Gene to desist by pulling a gun on him and the other man was taken to get stitches in his head. In the excitement, Gene hopped a train for New York. He left owing approximately twenty five hundred dollars in unpaid debts.

He also left behind a legacy of legends. Someone said he had robbed a bank in Belen, New Mexico. He had a warrant out against him in Lincoln County, some claimed. Stories flew hot and thick. Probably some of them were true. The New Mexico legend that he had to stay away until the statute of limitations ran out was pure bunkum. In New Mexico the statute of limitations does not run while a person is out of the state.

The twenty years he stayed away from New Mexico were probably nearly as hard on Gene as a similar jail term might have been. Never a minute passed that he did not yearn to be released from his self imposed sentence and return.

Tularosa N.M. June 8th, 1902

My dear Lummis:

Am very busy, and will not have time to work over that Wildcat Thompson story till about July 20- Will then do the best I can for you. Am restrained from dithyrambics by consideration for Mr. Thompson, as this thing occurred much as stated a few months ago. And if I put in very much hysterics the cowpunchers would arise as one and laugh W. Thompson out of the country.

I enclose another Dundee story for consideration, with stamps. *I also send you M.S.S. verses which I probably like better than any one else ever will in as much as they constitute a full and complete biography of yours truly. Fear you will find them doubly unavail- able, as they were published without my knowledge, in the* Univeralist, *some five or six years ago. I send them on the off chance.*

With regards to Mrs. Lummis
Yours truly
Eugene Manlove Rhodes

P.S. Condolences are in order. My wife has gone on a six months visit to N.Y.

E.M.R.

Please explain to me about copyright. When you buy M.S.S. does that give you complete ownership with exclusive right to publish in book form or to suppress entirely? I ask this because I may take into my head to be somebody as is somebody after a while.

I am sending your subscription dep't a few subscriptions, also the names and addresses of several New Mexico people who would be desirable agents. Have also written to those people and explained to them that they were to introduce Out West *into these dark lands.*

> *With best wishes*
> *Yours truly*
> *Eugene M. Rhodes*

Roswell, N.M. May 17, 1905

My dear Lummis:

Have just read of your father's death in current issue of Out West. *Pray accept my profound sympathy.*

Of course I did not know of this when I inflicted my affairs on you. Am very sorry I intruded at such a time.

> *Yours truly*
> *Eugene M. Rhodes*

June 22nd, (190)5

Dear Rhodes:
 It is not unforgivable at all, but bad judgement. That's what I get for a prosperous outside. As a matter of fact I have not $50 in the world and do not expect it, and am $2000 in the hole and a good bit of it biting me. You seem to have all sorts of bad luck and I wish I could lift up on it; but I could not even help my own father. I will take the matter up with Moody and see if there is any balm in Gilead, but I guess we are all close winded.
 I have endless confidence in you and would send the hard coin at once if I had it; but I am probably a good deal worse bedeviled than you are to find it for myself.
 I am sorry the Roswell venture turned out so hollow; for I had considerable hopes of it according to the forecast you gave me.
 But keep a stiff upper lip. They do not hang nor even imprison for debt. Let Smith walk the floor for a while and you will be able to pay out. Meanwhile, if I can do anything to help I shall be more than glad to do so.
    Your friend,
    Chas. F. Lummis

Gene had written Lummis to ask for a loan of $50 against future stories, to pay off one of his many debtors. Lummis, as was often the case, was in financial straits himself. The reference to Roswell has to do with Gene's assurance that he would be hired as the editor of the Roswell *Daily Record,* a position he badly wanted. The owner turned him down.

 Lummis considered Gene a protege. Every letter he wrote him seemed full of encouragement, affection and fatherly concern, and, quite often contained very practical advice.

Chapter 5

Apalachin Confinement

Gene arrived at Apalachin with May's guitar, a rug she cherished and three dollars in his pocket along with a bundle of finished, unfinished and rejected manuscripts. The next day he began a fifteen year sentence as a poor dirt farmer in 6 inches of late spring snow.

Gene never adjusted to the change in environment. The abrupt change from the desert to the rolling hills of upper New York and especially the extreme change of climate, was a shock he never got over. He felt boxed in. "Crated" was the term he used. Especially when the snow drifted 8 feet deep and the temperature dropped to -27 degrees and stayed there for a week.

And the people: their customs, traditions, habits, all products of an old stratified society, grated on Gene's free spirit.

Gene could see that what was happening to his beloved Southwest had already happened to this benighted land long before. He voiced his awareness and deep concern three quarters of a century before society in general became awakened. In a fiction story, "Over, Under, Around and Through," in the *Saturday Evening Post,* April 21-May 19, 1917, he wrote, speaking of both New Mexico and New York, "We have given away our coal, the wealth of our past, our oil, the wealth of today; except we do presently think to some purpose, we shall give away our stored electricity, the wealth of the future—our water power, which should, which must remain ours and our children's."

One of the most difficult adjustments Gene had to make was to the routine of daily living in a house, surrounded by his family. After his childhood days on the Nebraska and Kansas prairies, his home had mostly been under his hat. His parent's home, his own boar's nest at the ranch, even the house he rented for May, had been mostly jumping off places to his next adventure.

He did immediately establish a strong bond of respect and affection for May's father, Lucius Davison. Tall, gentle, gaunt, well educated and in his seventieth year, Lucius was a man Gene could and did admire.

Years later, Gene wrote, "He is a pleasant memory to me. Absolute integrity and good will and kindness. My affection for him has never waned and I miss him sorely."

Gene also felt genuine affection for sixty-nine year old Mrs. Davison but they were both set in their ways and small frictions did arise.

Gene also established close ties with Jack and Fred, May's boys. They insisted upon taking his name, although he never legally adopted them.

Alan, his own son, became very much like Gene. Gene had said once that he hoped his son, "Would stick with dogged perserverence to whatever he undertook." Later, he was forced to eat those words. "You cannot tell that boy anything. He gets an idea into his stubborn head and all Hell can't drive it out."

The great tragedy of his life, which occurred in the early years at Apalachin, nearly destroyed Gene. He never fully recovered. His second child, Barbara, was born on February 19, 1909. She lived only 20 months, a victim of diabetes. Gene doted on her, was her constant companion from the time it became evident that she was ill. In his anguish, he wrote to his mentor and staunch supporter, Charles Lummis.

Apalachin, N.Y. Oct. 25 (1910)

Dear Lummis:

   Our little Barbara left us yesterday. The one whose photograph I sent you was twenty months old—born on the birthday of one of our boys and died on the birthday of another.

   It was diabetes—and we have known for some days that there was no hope. Friday my wife spoke to me of the letter you wrote me when you lost your little one. (Lummis' firstborn son, Amado, had died Christmas Day, 1900, age six, of pneumonia) and what you wrote of it in Out West *and we have spoken and thought of it so often since. I have the letter and did keep that number of* Out West *but may not have it now. But we remember and it has been a help.*

   My three wild wayward boys were all good to Barbara, and all loved her dearly. We were all together on the old farm—a merry and happy summer and she was the life and heart of it for all of us. She was brave and merry and gay and sturdy and jolly. She was desired and welcome. I have not been able to write my stories for months and I am so thankful now, because I put in almost every hour with her as play fellow and caretaker.

   We are going to be sensible and keep her place in the circle, keep our memory of all her pretty baby ways for a blessing and a comfort and a joy and not make grief a curse. We will speak freely of her and not give up to bitterness and rebellion. Such a great style of baby, her mother said.

   We will not put her memory away in the corroding dark but keep her place bright and be grateful that she stayed so long to try to bear out what would have shamed her had she lived. There have many shames and dishonors stained my life, and every one of them now makes it easier to bear her leaving us, for she is beyond the reach of time. You know, I have no creed but I know it must be well with the child that is past uncertainty or doubt. No fear. and the sorrow is not for her, of course—life is not so sweet —but for us—she was brave and gritty above all things, first of all, and then merry and gay—and it would not become her mother and her dad to be quitters. so we'll just do the best we can and keep going. - And welcome life back again and not shrink from laughter when it comes but be glad knowing she would be glad if she knew. It has been a wonderful twenty months, too good to last - But the light of it and the joy of her will stay with us.

> *Your friend*
> *Rhodes*

Of Gene's grief, May wrote:

"Barbara died on Fred's birthday, October 24, 1910. She was Gene's idol. I really thought he would lose his mind with grief. He never completely recovered. We stood beside her wasted colorless form in the dimness of the small bedroom where her body had been placed in front of the open window with the blinds closed. Gene turned the slats of the blinds and let the pale October sunshine fall on her.

"She will be shut away from the sun so long," he said, his voice hoarse with grief.

He wrote a little letter to God, telling Him her favorite games, that she like to help, and would he put her in the care of some very motherly angel. Dry eyed, we both signed it. We were too cursed for tears."

Later that year, Gene started a story, "The Brave Adventure", dedicated to Barbara; a story of the Civil War. It was published in 1917 by *Redbook,* much abridged.

The early years on the farm at Apalachin, although Gene complained bitterly about his confinement there, were a combination of the hardest physical labor and a relatively productive time of writing.

After Barbara's death, May and Gene and the boys rented a house in Apalachin and stayed there for two years. In 1912, they bought a farm nearby and remodelled to suit themselves.

A home of their own relieved much of the stress that plagued Gene. Trying to write in a rather small farm house shared by four adults, three boys, and a baby had been trying, to say the least.

Gene's early stories published in *Out West* aroused the interest of Henry Wallace Phillips, an author whose stories, laid primarily in the Northern Plains, were already well known to regular readers of *Saturday Evening Post, Munsey's* and *McClure* magazines. Phillips had been a commercial illustrator but turned to writing under the urging of Rupert Hughes, a prominent author of the time. Phillips' stories were witty, uproariously humorous, done with a distinctive style and much in demand.

Gene and Phillips collaborated on a number of stories. Gene would provide a plot, scene and incident and Phillips would prepare the raw material for publishing. While Gene received neither pay nor by-line credits, he gained a wealth of experience from the partnership.

Emerson Hough, grand old man of the plains, and popular "Western" novelist, met with Gene on a material gathering expedition through southern New Mexico with Pat Garrett in 1904. Hough greatly encouraged Gene in his literary efforts and won Gene's staunch support in later years when "New Age" literary critics were, to Gene at least, maligning Hough's writings as shallow and unrealistic tales "designed to flabbergast."

The first years at Apalachin, in spite of having to learn to be a farmer, were among Gene's most productive. He hadn't much more than moved in when he was off to New York City to visit Henry Wallace Phillips in his home on Staten Island. They soon polished up four stories Gene had brought with him from New Mexico and sold them for $175.00.

Gene was first published by *Saturday Evening Post* with a story he and Phillips wrote together, "The Numismatist". It appeared in the March 22, 1907 issue. Within three years Gene's stories were being published by the most widely read magazines in America and his star had begun to rise. He still made contributions to *Out West, Pacific Monthly,* and the early *Sunset,* which was at that time a literary magazine. Gene always remained a magazine story writer. His books all began as short stories and were padded and expanded out to book bulk.

Even with these successful efforts, Gene never let his writing interfere with his duties on the farm, onerous though they might be. Stock had to be tended and fed, fields prepared, planted, harvested. Fences had to be kept up, manure had to be shoveled. Gene wrote, farmed, raised his family, helped care for May's aging parents, and pined for New Mexico. It goes to the plus side of Gene's ledger that he never complained, was as gentle with May's parents as he would have been with his own and that he never allowed the farm to become run down.

Chapter 6

Lost In Los Angeles

For thirteen years, from 1906 to 1919, Gene Rhodes settled into the harness of respectability. As W. H. Hutchinson wrote, "A trembling Pegasus hitched to a plow, a mustang stallion broke to look through a collar." He loved May and learned to be aware of her needs. He raised his boys and must have been a wonderful father. He dealt with the myriad problems a poor dirt farmer faces; the weather, the rocky soil, the poor quality of seed, the machinery breakdowns, the stock, the rise and fall of the market. And he wrote. What the land failed to provide, the income from his stories supplied. Affluence was always a stranger but needs were met and bills got paid.

Not a day passed that Gene did not mourn. First for his lost Barbara, then for his beloved New Mexico. Increasingly, his mother began to creep into his thoughts. She had greatly influenced Gene in his younger years; had in fact dominated the whole family, with her energetic and forceful personality. Now she wrote regularly, hinting of advancing age's aches and pains, and it troubled Gene to think of the possibility of her dying so far away in California while he labored here in New York state. Actually she was in excellent health, given her age, 76, living with three other women in a house at 4547 Marmion Way in the Arroyo Seco, not far from Charles Lummis' fabled stone house, El Alisal, and about a city block from the Southwest Museum.

Gene convinced himself that he should see his mother one more time. He also became convinced that he could sell film rights to some of his stories, which he in fact did. He began to make plans to go to California. His first plan involved a six month's stay in Los Angeles and a return via New Mexico where he could prepare for a serial he had in mind. The aspect of such a trip after the years on the farm must have seemed like a bright spot of sunshine on a dreary day to Gene.

Perhaps May approved. No one could have faulted Gene for the selfless effort he had made to make farming work or the loyalty he had shown to her mother and father since 1906. Perhaps she saw a need in Gene for spiritual and mental refreshment. What questions arose in her mind about caring for, and supporting, her family without Gene's presence, no one will ever know. A recent severe bout with influenza had left Gene with a permanently damaged heart. Perhaps she wanted him to get away and rest. What we do know is that on November 25, 1919, *Saturday Evening Post* bought "Stepsons of Light" and within three weeks Gene was on his way.

Early in 1920 Gene arrived in Los Angeles. He stayed for a short time with his niece, Hilda, daughter of Gene's brother Clarence, and her family in the Boyles Heights district.

They were preparing to move to Mexico to join Clarence and offered the house to Gene to buy. Gene thought it would be ideal for a home for him and his mother, but Julia would have none of it. She would not consider moving. The upshot was that Gene moved into a converted hen house in the rear of the house on Marmion, an arrangement that was not conducive to creative concentration. Every time Gene appeared about to write something, his mother was prone to exclaim: " Thank Heaven! At last you are going to write, "whereupon Gene would do something else, usually somewhere else.

Gene's voluntary exile, originally planned to last for just over 6 months, actually lasted 3 years. He sold the film rights to 3 stories for a total of $7500.00. He received $750.00 from his story, "Hit the Line Hard". He also added to his income with small royalties from book sales. This had to be divided between his living expenses, those of his family in New York and demands made upon him in Los Angeles. The primary reason he stayed away for 3 years was that he simply couldn't raise the train fare home.

During Gene's absence, May's boys left the farm and married. Alan got a job in Binghamton, a bustling industrial city twenty miles east of Apalachin. May's mother fell and broke her hip. She remained an invalid for the rest of her life. May moved back into her parent's farm, converted an old horsebarn into a henhouse and gradually built up a flock of laying hens to supplement what little income Gene was able to send home.

The nagging worry and the guilt Gene felt about leaving May to fend for herself, as well as his own very insecure finances did not help the creative juices to flow. He wrote, reluctantly, but not a single book or story did he publish during that three year hiatus. He did get a few articles published in "movie magazines" such as *Photoplay,* and *The Photodramatist,* and he remained, as ever, highly distractible.

The high points in his life consisted primarily of visiting with friends who lived in the Arroyo Seco. Charles Lummis, his old friend and ex-editor, Will Levington Comfort, author of *Apache,* James Willard Schultz, prolific writer of boy's Indian books and Harry Carr, editor of the *Los Angeles Times,* and author of *The West is Still Wild,* all lived nearby and gathered often. In addition, Gene met regularly with another group made up of Will Rogers, Charlie Russell, Henry H. Knibbs, Schultz and E. A. Brininstool, western history writer. Western fiction writer W. C. Tuttle, himself the son of a Montana sheriff, and Charles Siringo were frequently visited by Gene for "bull sessions" about the West-that-was.

Perhaps the most productive, and certainly one of the warmest friendships Gene established in Los Angeles was with movie actor Harry Carey and his wife Olive. Carey had taken lead roles in films made from Gene's books. He was a dyed-in-the-wool Rhodes fan. They became close friends. Gene spent many happy hours at the Carey ranch north of Los Angeles as well as at the studio, working as a consultant with Harry. In the end it was the Careys who rescued Gene from Los Angeles.

Feb. 10, 1920

My dear Gene:

I am busily engaged filming your "Desire of the Moth", which Universal made four or five years ago with Monroe Salsbury in the part of Foy, but after carefully re-reading your novel, I was— wot you call 'im? sort of nonplussed. I couldn't find a dang bit of similarity in the two tales and thereupon, moreover and Whereas I being a great admirer of your literature (for that's just what it is) I girded up my loins and set about really making your story as I thought you would like to have it made. But I am not playing the part of Chris Foy.

I do not like the name Foy, for I was once stuck on a chorus girl that worked for Eddie Foy. John Wesley Pringle is my kind of man. I mean the kind of "Outwester" I like to play. He smells of greasewood smoke and Bull Durham instead of tanbark and billposting paste.

Now to the point. Jack Ford, my director, and myself want you to come out to the studio the day we do the saloon sequence where they frame up on Foy. We think you ought to come and indulge in a medicine talk about this picture and some future ones, I want you to meet a couple of people anyhow.

Olive will let you know the day before we do the aforesaid sequence.

> *Adios, (Harry Carey)*

Carey wrote this letter, taken from W. H. Hutchinson's *A Bar Cross Man,* just a month after Gene had arrived in Los Angeles. It seems to indicate that Gene and Carey had had prior correspondence. It also hints at the high regard Carey held toward Gene's writing. The director Carey speaks of as Jack Ford, is better known to today's movie goers as John Ford.

Turbesé Lummis Fisk

Another alliance, and a great solace to Gene during his exile, was his close relationship and constant correspondence with, Turbesé Lummis Fiske, only daughter of Charles Lummis, Gene's mentor and friend. Frequently they wrote to each other two and three times a day.

Turbesé, born to Charles and his second wife Eva, during their stay at Isleta, New Mexico, in June, 1892, was in her late twenties. She was living in San Francisco, married to Frank Fiske, reporter for the San Diego *Sun,* who later became night editor for the San Francisco *Chronicle.* They were beginning to go their separate ways when Gene arrived in Los Angeles. Turbesé's greatest ambition was to become an actress; she was in fact working as an extra in a play in San Francisco when Gene arrived in Los Angeles.

Gene's salutation at the head of most of the letters he wrote to Turbesé, was "Dear Little Extra:. His other favorite term for her was "Dear Quaints", which well suited her.

Turbesé had spent her childhood and youth under the shadow of a dominant, self-absorbed father of eccentric and flamboyant ways and seemed determined to develop her own free spirit. She had known Gene since she was a small girl. He had been in the Lummis home many times while she was growing up. Their letters, while Gene was stranded in Los Angles, were warm, intimate and affectionate. It has been suggested that perhaps they were involved in an affair of the heart, which would have been a logical assumption. Both she and Gene were romantics to the core; she and Mr. Fiske were no longer close, and Gene was a very lonely, unhappy refugee. Turbesé was totally devoted to those she cared for.

There are some very good reasons why that assumption is probably in error. Gene was in his early fifties, in poor health, while Turbesé was still in her twenties. Gene, while he undoubtedly had sown wild oats in his youth, was now too puritanical in his attitudes toward love, sex and infidelity to ever let himself be drawn into anything that would compromise his loyalty and devotion to May. Certainly he was tempted. It seems likely, however, that Turbesé was teasing; that she saw Gene as a lonely avuncular figure in need of attention and set out to cheer him up in the only way she knew how.

That Gene was weighted with guilt is evidenced by a letter he sent to Turbesé shortly after arriving back in New York.

'Dear quaints and wistful ghost:
—I am a long lifetime older than you. It was and is up to me to give you a lead—not to wait for you to make all decisions. So I thought—still think that another dream city correspondence could but lead to disaster; adding fuel to two conflagrations already sufficiently raging.
—this is shabby to that lovely lady (May) to write this. Caddish, I reckon. But I cannot leave you torturing yourself with purely imaginary griefs—when there is so much real and un-get-aroundable cause for despair.
—quaints, she (May) has been a prisoner and slave. For two years not only single ray of joy, or pleasure. No rest, little sleep—

Immediately Gene began to make plans for the move back to New Mexico, but poor health, lack of money and the monumental task of closing down and selling the farm wiped out the better part of a year before they were ready to leave. Finally their Huppmobile, beginning to show signs of aging, was loaded and the Rhodes were on their way west. Their first stop was in West Virginia to visit Fred. From there, they made their leisurely way to Santa Fe, New Mexico.

Why Gene elected to settle in Santa Fe is a mystery. Gene's old stomping grounds were far south of there. Santa Fe, and its neighbor, Taos, were beginning to fill up with eastern artists and writers, the famous and soon-to-be famous who were entranced with the beauty and simple lifestyle of the Southwest, but it was not Gene's territory and he evidenced no interest in joining the artist colony. His one close contact in Santa Fe was Alice Corbin Henderson, the poet. She and her husband, William Pennhallow Henderson, greeted the Rhodes warmly and helped them settle in.

Gene's niece, Jean Rhodes, was living in Santa Fe at the time. Perhaps she persuaded Gene to try Santa Fe as a home base. Whatever the reason, Gene soon learned it was not the place for him. He wandered the Plaza and the narrow streets in a rumpled old brown suit and seemed completely out of place. The folly of staying in Santa Fe soon became apparent to both Gene and May. It was too high, too cold, too costly for their ever shrinking purse.

In September 1927, the Rhodes moved to Alamogordo, New Mexico. Now, it would seem, Gene had finally come home and could comfortably live out the remainder of his life among old friends. They rented a house across the street from Oliver Lee, and Gene and Oliver spent many happy hours reminiscing. But this too, was not to last. Gene was hard pressed to come up with the rent money. In fact, the landlord rented the place out from under the Rhodes, to a schoolteacher with a steady job. Gene and

May were saved from being evicted by ex-senator Albert Bacon Fall, who was still endeavoring to clear himself of the bribery charges made against him during the infamous Teapot Dome scandal. Senator Fall still had control of most of his Hatchet Cattle Company. Among his holdings was the Rock House, a huge stone structure at White Mountain, twelve miles from Three Rivers, New Mexico.

The house had at one time been the residence of Susan McSween, widow of Alexander McSween, one of the major participants—and victims of the Lincoln County War. Gene had been a staunch supporter of Fall. Now the Rock House was empty and was turned over to the Rhodes, rent free. This arrangement lasted until November, 1929, when Fall's property was sold. The Rhodes then bought three acres and a house which had not been lived in for years. It took Gene two months to make it habitable and to clear out the rattlesnakes.

Now it began to become clear to Gene and May, that life in New Mexico, beautiful though it was, was too hard to deal with on a day-to-day basis. The simple problems of shopping, heating the house and supplying water drained Gene's time and strength. The wind and dust plagued their lungs and Gene's heart. May became increasingly apprehensive about being so isolated. She was also beginning to have serious trouble with her eyesight. Sadly, reluctantly, Gene came to the realization that his beloved homeland was no longer a healthy place for them to live. The grief he felt over this decision must have been shattering after the years of longing to return.

In the summer of 1930 they made a trip to Southern California searching for a place to live. They found it in Pacific Beach, just outside San Diego. They returned home and Gene buckled down to write a long enough story to pay their debts and make the move possible. He wrote a spirited essay in protest of Walter

Noble Burns' character mutilation in his sensational, but histori-cally inaccurate *Saga of Billy the Kid.* He sold it to *Sunset Magazine.* He wrote a stirring appreciation of his friend Charles A. Siringo, author of *Riata and Spurs.* He sold a story, "Maid Most Dear", to the *Saturday Evening Post* and four short stories to *Cosmopolitan Magazine.* He also sold two ballads to *Adventure Magazine.*

In July 1930, Gene started *The Trusty Knaves.* He finished it and sent it to the *Saturday Evening Post* in February 1931. They sent him back a check for $7,500 less advances and at the end of February May and Gene were enroute to California and the end of Gene's trail. He consoled himself by asserting that the move was only to escape New Mexico winters and that they would divide their time between New Mexico and California. It never happened. Other than a few brief trips, mostly to close the sale on their house, Gene and May resided in Pacific Beach, until the end.

Tesuque, Santa Fe, Ja. 4 (1927)

Dear Don Carlos:

There is no P.O. by name of Tesuque. Your letter went to St. Louis and has just reached us. Letters must be addressed to Tesuque Santa Fe.

Hope you are better. May is: but I am in dreadful shape. Twenty four hours after we get some money to go on, we are off to a month at the Hot Springs (Palmas). Hence to Alamogordo or Tularosa. It is suicide for me to stay here. I am worse and feebler every day. Can't possibly live here. Sorry: I like it better here than any place I've ever seen,—except for heat. It has been bitter with a deep snow.

Love to all for now. Your Gene Rhodes

Tesuque, Santa Fe, N.M., Jan. 6, 1927

Dear friend:
I forgot to say that when my money comes, I will send you that
$50. Also that I haven't got my car yet. Am out $53 on it so far and
it is in worse shape than when it went into shop. Fortunately, Mr.
Fahy loaned me his car, so we have not been afoot.
May came down with tonsillitis <u>again</u> last night, and she has it
bad this time. She wasn't able to get up; and when she fails to
come up smiling, that means a mighty sick woman. That settles
it; we light out for the south at earliest possible moment; as soon
as she is able to take train; and as soon as I get some money ... As
to this last, I have been shamefully treated by four several men,
not counting Mr. Fly, my erstwhile publisher, who does not
qualify as a man. At that, I think enough will come along to serve
my needs; have had earnest promises...not, however, current with
the merchant.
May sends love, and we both hope that you are doing better
than we are. Item, do not forget Abdul.
Yours truly, and with New Year Greetings,
Gyp the Blood

The reference to Mr. Fly relates to Gene's one adventure with
the H. K. Fly Publishing Company. They had published his
novel, *West is West*, with almost six hundred typographical
errors, an inauspicious beginning to a relationship that went
rapidly downhill from there.

Gene was taken with a popular humorous song of the time,
named "Abdul Abulbul Amir". He had heard it sung at Lummis'
home and Lummis had promised to send him the words. Thus the
reminder not to forget Abdul. In a later letter, he related that he

and May had purchased a phonograph and that the first record they had bought was "Abdul Abulbul Amir".

Charles Lummis responded to these two letters as follows:

Dear Old Indigo Jake:-
I have yours of the 4th and the 6th; and am dropping all other things to put on my surgeons apron and take my broad ax and saw, and start to prescribe!
I suppose you have already let minor cut ups relieve you of the commonly recognized sources of system poison. That they have drug out your teeth each with a rattlesnake at its root; and your tonsils, a pair of Hooded Cobras; and that little Pichuacuate known as the appendix.
But all of these are relatively minor matters when it comes to circulating venom in the system; and I am going after the fountainhead of all the poison.
You are as brave a man in many ways, as wise a man; in nearly every way, as loveable a man—and redeemed in most aspects of life by a real sense of Humor.
But you have gotten into the habit of Gloom—which is positively ridiculous. You know that I do not underestimate the cruel adversities you have suffered—you know also that I have had enough of my own to have a reasonable standard of measures, and that I am not one of those cheerful idiots who never felt or never suffered and who greet you in a grave affliction with a simper and then says, "cheer up—the worst is yet to come."
You do not realize in the least what a hold this Habit has on you, nor what it is doing to you. Your rare letters of the last years have impressed me with this conviction; but the time I spent with you in New Mexico this Season gave me a pretty thorough size-up.
Gloom and Despondency are worse poisons for the health

than ever lay in teeth or tonsils or appendix; and I have never seen such an erebus of Gloom as I found you. *It is in your tone, your walk, your everything—you are as thorough going and consistent a Despondent as I ever saw.*

And dear old Gene it is not worthy of you! It is cowardly and you are not a coward, it is foolish and you are not a fool. It is absolutely lacking in Humor, and you have a fine sense of Humor about everything else. It isn't fair to that wonderful May of yours, and I concluded that probably no other woman in the world, would have stood you so long, and my hat is off to her. Her only fault is that she has not taken a club to you!

Fly and the other cheap publishers who have robbed you of a little money, or of a good deal, have not lost you a tenth part as much as you have lost yourself. If you would do less worrying about them and write more for those who won't rob you, several of your problems would be solved. I would gladly join you in a hemp party to elevate robber publishers; but in the meantime all that I can do is to use the rope's end for a little attention to their embittered victim.

I did not tell you anything about my own predicament, which you would readily admit is incomparably worse than yours; but it does not make me bitter, though the circumstances are far more aggravated. My head isn't in half as good shape as yours, nor my health; and I am facing permanent blindness not far off—and a great many other things. But I am never despondent.

This is not because I am braver than you, for I am not, nor wiser than you, nor with the human companionship with which you are blessed, it is simply that I happen to see the Joke, and never get into that Habit of Self-pity or resentment.

And you have unconsciously gotten into that Habit—which is humiliating, and God knows you have had enough to confirm you in it.

But it's all in the point of view. Stop Kitty from running around a minute, and think as soberly as you can whether this Gloom habit is getting you anywhere, whether it is helpful to May, or anyone else that loves you, above all whether it is a good tonic for your own system.

I have had as much reason to hate as many people as you have and do; but a good many years ago I discovered that while I was hating Hell out of them, and lying awake nights to do it, they were peacefully snoring and getting fat and I was not doing a thing but burning myself up; since which Dawn of Intelligence, I have never hated anyone. These tactful remarks are not because I have nothing else to do. That absconding Secretary who left two days before my return, has left things in a frightful mess; and my eyes are like a steady tooth-ache probably trying to get too much done.

But I love you and value you and therefore feel free to insult you thus effectively, in a faint hope that I may awaken a spark of almost human intelligence in you, as to yourself. If you get mad at me it will be a much more healthful rage, than any of the many that have been wearing your heart out for several years. I ought to have talked it out with you while there; but while my impressions are quick, my judgments are slow and I wanted perspective on the thing. Now I have it. Now you have it.

Give my love to May. She is God's pattern of a woman. I hope her bronchitis is permanently relieved, still more that she is relieved of the dark blue cloud over the Spirit of the Man she loves, and has so nobly cared for.

You will do nothing of the kind with that check.

Sorry the Old Car has a grouch also—see what you have done even to the inanimate!

Sorry if you have to leave Tesuque. It is a lovely place, and would love to have it myself, but it is hardly a winter resort. Keep me advised of your changes of address—that is, if and when

I am enough forgiven to be trusted with your Post Office.
I note what you say about Hagermann and the Pueblo Council; and will talk to Collier about it. On its face it is good.
With all love and best wishes—and Dammit, SNAP OUT OF THAT!
Always your friend,(Charles Fletcher Lummis)

Gene's response to Lummis' scolding was as follows:

Tesuque, Jan. 17, '27

My dear Abdul;
Right. Move up three girls. I must pocket my losses and erase them from the ledger.
Yessir; I have been plumb poisoned by the incessant desire for the blood of a Yiddishman. Some not inconsiderable part of my standing grouch was for the sorrows of others; perhaps less ignoble, but not less unwise than the resentment born of my own idiocies. Neglecting fractions then, you are hideously correct, and I thank you for a noble letter.
I have a fairish idea of your trouble, but confess to naked cowardice. At the time, I was perplexed to the limit by the several distresses of each of my three—count'em, three (3) several sons; and I didn't feel I could bear any more; was sure I would squeal like a pig. If I had any pull I would say a little prayer for you.
We are trying to find tenant to take this lease off our hands. We have signed contract binding us until May first, and hate to pay double rent. Three urgent letters of inquiry as to present conditions in Alamogordo bring no results. Even real estate men won't answer. Howdumsoever, know about essentials; everything except the cost part.
We like Santa Fe better than ever, and hate to go. More

intelligence per capita than any place I know.
May sends her love. We are both better,
Gratefully,
Ivan Petroffsky Scovar

May answered in her habitual calm and gentle style.

Dear Dr. Lummis:
I thank you for viewing my extremely ordinary virtues through
such powerfully magnifying rose glasses. I am filled with awe
and admiration at the thoughts of what a wonderful woman I
would be if I could come up to your estimate of me, but it was lovely
of you to say those things and I cannot remember when I have been
so rarely pleased. It must have been the effect of those waffles!
That was a marvelous letter you wrote Gene.
You are truly in a class by yourself, and I am filled with the
most profound admiration at not the grim way, but the gallant
way in which you are facing blindness, as if you virtually defied
fate to do her worst.
I am hoping it may not prove as serious as it seems, for with
your exceptional constitution backed by My Friend Will, the
chances are an even thousand to one that an operation would be
successful, and they need only operate on one eye at a time, and it
isn't a painful operation.
We want you to come back and see us again sometime, and
sing about Araby's daughter, and Heaven is my home. You sang
beautifully and it was a great treat.
With all the good wishes in the world.
With love
Your friend,
May Rhodes

May certainly had reason to know about eye problems. At the time she wrote this letter she was suffering from the combined results of years of transcribing Gene's abominable handwriting and rapidly progressing cataracts. Her love and patience seem to reflect from every word. She suspected that blindness was in the offing. She was right, but fortunately it did not come until some time after Gene's death.

Charles replied with a gentle rebuke, and more advice.

Jan. 24, 1927

Dear May;

That is a beautiful letter; but young women should not tell whitehaired men, be it ever so politely, that they "don't know what they are talking about" and are not competent judges. But I knew you did not mean to be sassy, so the disrespect is forgiven. And of course I could not possibly be anything else but forgiving to the lady who says that I "sang beautifully". And while I could not recommend you consciously as a Music Critic to the Mercury I very much prefer you in that capacity for my own case to any that Mr. Mencken ever hired. I shall hope to come under your roof tree somewhere sometime, and sing until the cows come home!

Gene's answer to my devilish assault is fine and manful, and warms my heart. All these things are simply the Point of View, when we see straight, we walk straight. Its only when we get cross-eyed or zig-zag that we wobble off into the wrong path. If I believed that a decent and polite letter would have made Gene think, that's the kind I would have written; but most of us need to be knocked between the eyes, and perhaps beaten up a bit before we get the thought. I think he has it now, but I think you will need to use the follow up system on him--which you can do so beautifully and without nagging. One of the rarest traits in a wife.

*I am doubtful about this Alamogordo business, though thor-
oughly agreed that you both better get down to a lower altitude
and a warmer sky for the next three months or so. If I can get a
chance I will tell Gene what I think about this matter. It is a
matter not of climatology so much as psychology, just as Gene's
coffee and other troubles are ten times as much his nerves as any
chronic iniquity of his throat or lungs. Of course his cure lies
almost wholly in himself, but environment counts a little, and as
a Master Physician I should decidedly prescribe an environment
which would be soothing and interesting but perhaps not familiar—for the particular reason that the old and dear scenes when
revisited have about ten parts disappointment and irritation at
the unauthorized changes to one part of the glow of loving
memories.*

*God bless you both! I have loved Gene very deeply ever since
I first knew him by his youthful stories to my little magazine. I
count it a genuine happiness and memory to have found you, just
what one would wish his dear friend's wife to be.*

Now Hold Him Steady. With love and all good wishes.

Always your friend,

Two days after he wrote to May, Charles sent this advisory
epistle, to which warning Gene paid not the slightest heed. His
head was set. As it turned out, financially, the move to Alamogordo
was the right one since it ultimately secured the Rhodes a rent
free home for about two years.

Jan. 26, 1927

Good! Gallantly Spoken and again like Gene of mine:-

*Your sense of humor is not all gone yet; but trot it out and keep
it running—for you will need it right along to help you really to
break a long and vicious Habit.*

I savvy that your afflictions are largely for other people--but did you ever know of your helping them any better in their troubles by getting sick and disqualified for anything whatsoever. I have a pretty strong tie in my friendships, and grieve when my friends grieve—but I don't worry about it. On the contrary I find that by keeping cool I am much more likely to derive some practical means of being of use to them.

I hope you will find a tenant for the lovely little Ranch; for there is no question that both of you ought to get out of there for the winter months. The reason is partly climatic and equally psychological.

I am glad you appreciate Santa Fe—it is very much as you say— and a blessed old oasis of humanity in a Sorry desert of Civilization.

But discarding the surgeons apron and hack saw for the Materia Medica—I would suggest that you think at least three days (if you can do that much) before you go to Alamogordo or Tularosa—or any of the damn dear country you used to know. Go as low down, but to some country you don't know at all, but where your mental activities as to your environment will be all in adjusting yourself to new and interesting things—and where there will be no Disappointments of Comparison, and no tallys of Loss.

You ought to be old enough to realize that a man of your natural sensitiveness, now multiplied by the condition of your nerves and health till it is morbid and an actual disease—to go back to the country where you lived for a generation, a life that has absolutely disappeared during the years that you have been away is not to invite, but to command a chronic disappointment and mourning. For Tularosa, Gene, and all that country, wasn't the Geography, nor the sands, nor the rocks, nor the peaks, it was the life that you lived there. That life is no more. It's bad enough to find that most of the people are gone with whom you lived and loved and fought—but it is intolerable to find that the life itself is gone, which is all that through that glamour over the desert even a Stolid person like me would get into the State of resentment; and a well ripened boil of sensitiveness like you would (and not unjustifiably) hate and resent every damned stop of Progress and Change.

I am not a rash practitioner, but if I know anything about Human Nature, and about your subdivision thereof, the only wise thing for you to do is like the only wise thing for a person going back to the old Home in New England, visit it about one day; be piously sorry for the long roll of the dead; be gallant to the boyhood sweetheart who is fat and dowdy—and then pull your freight for somewhere else. But only a crazy man would think of living there.

You can get all the sweet memories out of that country in a week that it has left for you, after that every hour of every day will bring some aggravating at the Insolence of Time for meddling with your memories.

Get to someplace where you can learn something—besides new dirges for the Yesterdays and new anathemas for Today. You are making the mistake of your Senility and God knows you have no right to be senile. Your soul is full of Adventure—and that means the New. I have no stock in any resort of the Southwest— and have no idea whither to recommend you—unless it might be perhaps in the Salt River Valley in Arizona--away from Phoenix and other lunger towns, say up on Beaver Creek or Oak Creek in some of the little settlements where you and May could really Bask and Learn, and where you could work.

And then in July or August I hope you will be back in my country the two of you. And that you will take the thousand mile swing with Hewett and the International Congress of Americanists and me. The trouble with you is my dear boy, you never did know any desirable part of New Mexico! Let me have you for a month, in my old stomping ground. And you will be a different man!

May wrote me a beautiful letter, you both have been very gallant in this case of brutal assault and battery.

Just one damn thing after another here. Quimu* and his little family have to leave me in a week for at least six months, so I will be very much on My own. And today a very critical and anxious problem has arisen which I don't know what to do with, yet, but I shall muddle through it all as I always do.

God bless you both, and good luck—and that means your fault! Yes or no, we can't help what happens to us generally, but we can always help how we take it.

With love and all good wishes,

Always your friend,

(Charles Fletcher Lummis)

The following excerpt from Charles' letter to the Rhodes written June 14th, 1927, contains humorous comments about what he calls, "The Merry Madhouse" of Los Angeles, as well as an invitation to come and help Charles put together a volume of poetry he wanted to publish, and ultimately did, under the title, *The Bronco Pegasus.*

June 14, 1927
Mr. and Mrs. Eugene Manlove Rhodes
649 Galisteo Street
Santa Fe, New Mexico

Dear Gene and May:
I am still living in hope of getting over to New Mexico in August—tho God knows what on. I need it in my Business even after so short a term in this Merry Madhouse of Los Angeles. I don't know what the people do that live in the thick of it—I suppose

*Tiwa Indian name of CFL's eldest son, Jordan.

they just drivel. I keep away off at the side and still it makes me go in every day or two and look up at the old Sharp's Buffalo Gun and wish I had a few hundred rounds and to get up on my tower and turn loose for general results. Small danger of hitting anyone that didn't need it. If I come I hope to bring my secretary and the big camera, and get some more of my incomparable pictures, and some interviews with the few people left worth interviewing, and some other work done and I have a sudden hunch.

Always your friend
(Charles F. Lummis)

Three Rivers, N.M., Oct. 21, 1928

My Dear Abdul,
—Leussler was here two days and your ears must have burned.

Saw the dummy of The Bronco Pegasus *and it looks good. Heard also of your new book.* (Flowers of Our Lost Romance) *Hurrah for our side.*

Of course any letter that we can write now must leave the great thing unsaid—lacking the words.

You may be glad to know that May and I are flourishing like two bay horses. I had quite a spell with heart disease. So we moved up here to the very best place in New Mexico—the "Rock House" where Mrs. Barber lived. "Her as was" Mrs. McSween in the Lincoln County War. We are precisely at the base of the magnificent White Mountain, and we have as beautiful a view as the heart could wish for. Item, a well planned rock house, with walls two feet thick, five fireplaces, all ceilings twelve feet high, six rooms and bath, living room 18 x 30, and the others all 18 x something.

Item, wide hall (and living room in summer) right through the middle of the house. Item, wide screen in porch on three sides of the house. Item, running water, telephone, and sanitary plumbing. Item, A long row of gigantic mountain cottonwoods before the house, and behind it a magnificent walnut grove; Oak, elm, pine above oak, Juniper and cedar below the summit. It is just 5000 feet above us. We are here about 7000. Item, electric lights from a private power house, a mile away: so that we can cook one meal on the electric stove and the next in a Dutch oven on the fireplace. Item, soft water. Highest house on the creek: twelve miles from the post office: Alabama.

Well, as I was saying, the Doctor looked down his nose. So, I reformed. Worked with my fair hands, worked and walked and rode, a little and a little more. Pick, shovel, axe and hoe. Built irrigating ditches and wagon roads, chopped wood, hauled in and chopped it up, until now I do at least five hours hard manual labor every day, and snappy at that. Oftener eight or ten. We have four horses and we both ride persistently. Results: I have gained ten years or similar and May has lost many pounds: down to 165, that lady, and both of us feeling chipper.

Of course, there has not been very much doing in the literary line, but as I pointed out to Leussler when he grew garrulous, a corpse doesn't do any writing—and for the first time in many years my conscience is bright and clean. Oh yes, had to drop tobacco, meat and most all the coffee. Didn't mind. Queerly enough, I really like the diet that most people find so obnoxious. Spinach and such.

I thought you would like to hear all these things. Oh, yes: my book looks promising. (This was the book on New Mexican history that Gene never finished.)

Fine letter from Knibbs a day or two ago.

And now this thing I do not like to say. We wanted very much to come out and see you. The pocket book will not stand it.—for which I am very sorry.
   Yours lovingly,
    Gene

This letter, written a little over a month before Charles' death, indicates that Gene and May were well aware that Charles hadn't long to live. Probably Henry Knibbs, a close friend of both men, was keeping them informed. Gene was writing in such a newsy manner probably in an attempt to give Charles something to distract him from himself and his pain. It was very likely not an easy letter for Gene to write. He would never have used the term, Yours lovingly, to end such a letter if he had not been trying to convey a very real love to a very dear friend he felt certain he would never see again. In all likelihood, Charles had written to Gene, asking him to come and see him one more time.

Chapter 8

By the Shores of the Sundown Sea

In early 1931, Gene and May signed a trust deed note (no money down) to be paid in monthly installments of $18.53, interest included, for two twenty-five-foot lots at 914 Loring Street, in Pacific Beach, with —"a gray house of hollow tile and stucco." May wrote in *The Hired Man on Horseback*, "a huge eucalyptus tree hung guardingly over it, west of it lay the sea, and in front was a long line of surf beating on Mission Beach and Ocean Beach."

After much amused debate, the Rhodes agreed to call the house, "Eyore's House" because of Gene's affection for the works of A.A. Milne. This was later discarded in favor of "The Bimbles". In the end they gave up trying to find a name although Gene did propose that they name it "Belle Acres", with the second "e" firmly accented.

On the lot in back of the house, Gene added a small study with a large window facing the ocean. He installed a cot and an airtight wood stove. Other furnishings included a myriad of cigar boxes and tea boxes filled with notes on small scraps of paper— Gene's filing system. Here, Gene settled in to work until he could work no more.

Gene was deeply affected by what he saw of the effects of the depression in the San Diego area. In a letter to Theodore Van Soelen, he wrote, "Christmas cards stacked beside me. I do not like to send them. Yesterday, in La Jolla, an insensible man brought into the police station while I was there—visiting a cop who is a friend, I hasten to explain. As good a face as yours or mine. Starved. Somehow that helped me to see that tissue and tinfoil are not the same as the spirit of that dead man Christ who loved the luckless and the poor and wept for them. It put me out of conceit of Christmas cards. Also, the well groomed administration of welfare here treat the beneficiaries like dogs."

Gene played a little baseball when he felt up to it, umpired when he didn't, and when he was unable to do either, he worked at rounding up uniforms for the teams in his area. Baseball was to Gene what trout fishing was to Charles Lummis. He loved the sport but was seldom able to play.

Two serials, "The Proud Sheriff", and "Beyond the Desert" were published by *Saturday Evening Post* during this time. Gene wrote editorials for *Touring Topics,* a magazine published by the Automobile Club of Southern California. He spent a lot of time, which for him was quickly running out, writing on a project he had long held dear, a book about the old timers of New Mexico.

Another project demanding much time, and which proved a futile effort, was proposed to Gene by his old cronies of Arroyo Seco. It was to be *The Bar Cross Edition of the Works of Eugene Manlove Rhodes,* ten volumes, illustrated by Ed Borein and Maynard Dixon. The plan was to finance the project by subscriptions only, at $50.00 per set of 10 books. Gene felt the cost high but went ahead with this part of the venture. Not only did he rewrite his books, but he contacted many old friends in an effort to raise funds for the project, and to publicize it. It took 14 months for Gene and his friends to realize that the Bar Cross Edition was doomed. The funds could simply not be raised. Money was hard to come by in those early depression days.

And he wrote numberless letters. Letters to his publishing house to complain about how they were (not) publicizing his books, letters to authors whose books he admired, letters to editors, including the following, written to Thomas Costain, at that time associate editor of *Saturday Evening Post.*

November 27, 1933

Dear Mr. Costain:
    By this mail I am sending you a story—"Beyond the Desert"—48,000 words.
    I would appreciate it if you would kindly wire me decision. Sure, I know this is all foolishness. But this writing leaves me a tired man and I would sleep better if I knew the story suits you.
    Incidently, I have been six months writing this. Consequently, we are reduced to a diet of bread and sausage, and we are now heading for the last groundup.
                            Yours,
                    Eugene Manlove Rhodes

Gene and May shared 914 Loring with two kittens, Beppo and Damocles, who by mutual agreement ruled the house and the affectionate attention of two lonely, aging people who badly needed the distractions offered by a pair of bossy cats.

Of the circumstances surrounding the appeal of Costain, May wrote in *Hired Man on Horseback,* Gene's biography, "Gene was so weak and ill by now, and would often work all night on eight or ten pages, only to destroy them in the morning. "Beyond the Desert" progressed, but slowly. He was working with all his might to get the story done, which would pay off our debts and give us a slight balance. At last it was finished. He sent it off without return postage, because he didn't have it. We had exactly forty-eight cents in this world.

The Saturday Evening Post replied that they didn't want the story, but later accepted part of it and forwarded a cash advance, literally saving the Rhodes' bacon!

Gene's last published writing was a review of Ross Calvin's captivating book on New Mexico, *Sky Determines.* The day after the review appeared, Gene suffered a series of angina attacks. On June 26, 1934, he wrote to Calvin, congratulating him on his writings. That night he went to bed at one A.M. and suffered one spasm after another until morning. As dawn broke at half past six on the morning of June 27, Gene died in May's arms.

Of Gene's passing, E. Dana Johnson wrote in the Santa Fe *New Mexican:*

Good Man and True

"No phrase better describes the late Eugene Manlove Rhodes, who died yesterday in California, than the caption of one of his best loved books, defining the kind of men he glorified in a hundred tales of New Mexico—

"Good Men and True!"

"These men of his were a religion. They were largely unshaven, save at intervals. They wore battered, dusty old cow-hats. They were lean and had the permanent 'sun-grins'; they were grizzled and twinkly, or they were young and brown and buoyant and sang lustily as their ponies clattered through mountain passes or gully-slashed mesas or alkali flats. They were quiet, as a rule, humorous and happy and care-free and polite, addicted to practical jokes and good times around chuck wagon cook fires. But, when it came to putting something over on them or their friends; in matter of cheating, injustice to old men, or boys, or women; or meanness, or crooking, or crime, these men were hard, and stern, tireless, loyal and grim, courageous and resourceful.

"In every story, in every contribution to newspaper and every book, cropped out this religion of Gene Rhodes. His lance was lifted always against sham and pretense, and littleness and cowardice.

He hated dirt, he abhorred insincerity and hypocrisy.

The clean wind, the purple distances, the color and shimmering sunshine, the storms and rigors, the black lava and blue peaks of the land he loved and where he wanted to be buried; the beauty and the strength of the country called to him for men of like qualities. His creed was kindness, decency, simple stout heartedness. To these things he gave new vitality for millions of readers. In his own soul, he found the values of life on mountain tops, amid great distances, and among simple people herding cattle. His tales were imbued with the true genius of the Southwest. In New Mexico he was much loved largely because of the magic words in which he could say what so many of us feel about the country.

Quizzical, original, pungent, picturesque; range-rider, "desert rat," old-timer, contemporary of desperado and empire builder; fearless crusader, sentimental and beauty-loving, a cow-person and a born gentlemen; and a brilliant master of language, Gene Rhodes was A Good Man and True. He was New Mexico's truest interpreter and spokesman and he will always be enshrined in her heart."

On June 30, 1934, following the dictates of Gene's own wishes, May buried him in the San Andres mountains about two miles from his old horse ranch, where a pinion tree and two junipers would shade his grave.

Late that afternoon they covered his body, "Wearing with every scar, Honor at Eventide" in the rough white gypsum, and Gene became, for all time, a part of his beloved New Mexico.

Epitaph

Now hushed at last the murmur of his mirth,
Here he lies quiet in the quiet earth.
—When the last trumpet sounds on land and sea
He will arise then, chatting cheerfully,
And, blandly interrupting Gabriel,
He will go sauntering down the road to hell.
He will pause loitering at the infernal gate,
Advising Satan on affairs of state,
Complaining loudly that the roads are bad
And bragging what a jolly grave he had!

This epitaph, written by Rhodes, first appeared in May
Rhodes' biography, *The Hired Man on Horseback.*   It later
appeared in W.H. Hutchinson's *Little World Waddies.*

PART TWO

CHARLES FLETCHER LUMMIS, 1859-1928
The Stormy Petrel

Charles Fletcher Lummis, in the last decade of his life, wearing the medal of the Order of Isabela la Católica, presented to him by the king of Spain for his efforts to promote a positive view of Spanish culture.

Chapter 9

The Arrival

On a mild sunny day late in January, 1885, a lone man waited in a buggy at the end of the street in San Gabriel, California. A large, bearded man with a military bearing, he waited and watched the trail that came from the northeast and the foothills of the San Gabriel Mountains. As he waited, he occasionally lifted his watch from his waistcoat pocket, opened the case, consulted its face, snapped it shut and returned it to its proper place. He was not impatient. He was simply marking the passage of time, and watching.

Time passed gently. Birds fluttered and sang in tree branches overhead. In the shade, the drowsing team occasionally shook off flies or shifted their heavy hooves. Insects whirled and buzzed at their daily business. A small stream chuckled its way through a nearby orange grove. Motes of dust sparkled in the sun's soft light.

Then, late in the day, a slightly more dense dust cloud appeared far up the trail. Out of it there stepped a lean young man, his left arm in a sling, his clothing shabby and travel stained, his hat nearly white from trail dust. In spite of his somewhat bedraggled appearance, he moved with a self confident, almost jaunty gait, as though he were just completing a morning stroll.

He looked up as the waiting man stepped from his buggy and walked forward to greet him. With a warm smile, he grasped the other's hand in a firm, strong grip.

Thus, did Charles Fletcher Lummis complete a stroll that had begun in Cincinnati, Ohio, 143 days earlier, on September

12, 1884. He had walked over 3500 miles . He had survived unutterable hardships, pain, cold, hunger, loneliness. Except for the mending arm, he was in top physical condition.

The man who waited was Colonel Harrison Gray Otis, owner of the weekly Los Angeles *Times,* and Charles' new employer.

Together the two walked the eleven remaining miles into Los Angeles, and late that night, dined royally in a Hungarian restaurant. From there, Charles made his way to a hotel to greet his wife who had arrived ahead of him by train. The next morning, bathed and in clean attire, the first city editor of the Los Angeles *Times* was on the job.

Nobody knew it at the time, but this displaced New Englander was to become the Southwest's most impassioned spokesman. Through his eyes the nation would be made aware of the vast cultural, geological and archeological treasures contained in the states of New Mexico, Arizona and California. See America First! - he actually coined the phrase.

Chapter 10

Birth of a Stormy Petrel

Charles Fletcher Lummis came into the world on a cold windy day in early March, 1859, like a stormy petrel blown off course. He remained a stormy petrel his entire life.

Born in Lynn, Massachusetts, to a consumptive young mother who died following the birth of her second child two years later, and a brilliant educator father, Charles was so tiny and frail he was carried about on a pillow for the first six months of his life.

Following his mother's death, Charles was sent to live with his maternal grandparents in New Hampshire. There, for six years he explored his environment at first hand and provided much justification for the few spankings he received from his doting grandparents. He also was instilled with a passion for trout fishing by his grandfather, a small but extremely powerful man. Although in later years he had little time for fishing, the passion never faded. Even in those early years, there was much evidence of Charles' insatiable quest for knowledge, his thirst for exploration.

At age eight, Charles was returned to his father and enrolled in the primary class of the school of which his father was then principal. That lasted one day. Charles refused to go back and implored his father to teach him at home. Thus began an intensive instruction in Greek , Latin and Hebrew. There is no greater stimulus to a dedicated teacher than a willing, eager student. By the time he was seventeen, Charles could read the Bible in three languages and had read all the Latin and Greek literature on the Harvard elective list. Instruction in English grammar he never received or needed.

Charles' childhood was very much a lonely one. He had much time for introspection and little or no association with children of any age. Of necessity, he devised his own pasttimes, the major one being reading.

Early on, he was aware that he was small for his age, sickly, and somehow, "different," It is truly amazing how little families realize how much small children pick up from adult conversations. Charles determined to make the most of that difference. The embers of a fire glowed within him that few of us ever feel. It consumed him for sixty nine years.

Like any intelligent child who realizes his differences, be they physical or mental, Charles determined to prove his right to a position in society equal to or superior to his peers. That determination never left him. He not only yearned to gain status, but he burned for recognition from others.

This burning was a very real part of the fire that propelled him to such an illustrious list of accomplishments, and eventually, to physical collapse.

A lone child thinks long and deeply about himself. He is his own examining committee. In some family situations this can lead to a highly distorted self concept that is crippling to the person's entire life. In Charles, it inflamed his ego to enormous heights. Child of a caring father who gave him much undivided attention and support, he was indulged, loved, and praised. He had no siblings at home with whom he had to share his father's devotion. They remained close for the rest of his father's life. Charles grew, but not as fast as his self concept grew.

At eighteen, Charles entered Harvard; not because he was particularly eager, but because it was expected of him. His father was a Harvard graduate.

I had no personal ambition for college. I went because father had gone, because he had trained me with years of personal concentration. And because it was the cultural convention of New England—to which I acceded as I did in most things. Up until Harvard.

College in those days naturally meant Harvard. It was an intoxicating experience to enter a great university. I studied reasonably for my classes——What I needed, you see, was not so much to learn books as to Find Myself.

The time at Harvard was like strong sweet wine. Here he could apply all the notions he had held about himself to his experience with others. He became almost compulsive in his determination to develop his undersized body. He lifted weights, he boxed, he ran until he could run a twenty mile marathon with ease. Determined to prove his own superiority, he took on boxing partners who greatly outweighed him, taking much punishment on the chance of slipping in a stunning punch.

He fine tuned his small slim frame into a highly coordinated, lightning fast machine. A photograph taken of him on the parallel bars at Harvard shows a determined athlete with not a pound in his body that was not muscle, skin or bone.

At Harvard, Charles managed to get involved in some very typical freshman antics, most of which he survived without harm to his body or the Lummis name, and made some friends that were to remain friends for life. Principal among these was Theodore Roosevelt. Of him, Charles wrote;

There was an odd looking chap at Harvard. He was flat chested, thin necked, hatchet-faced, lantern-jawed. He wore funny thin Dundreary side whiskers, silky but innumerous. His name was Theodore Roosevelt.

I shall never forget the looks of him in those early college days. No photograph I have ever seen of him confirms it. The retouched

Freshman picture is as sharp as a cameo. About this stringy bantling, not more than an inch taller than my 5-ft-6 and much lighter than my 120, there was nothing whatever to suggest the powerful frame and world known forceful face of later years save the same glasses and the same teeth!

Theodore Roosevelt was a year ahead of Charles in Harvard and therefore they had no close contact while in school. But they shared many things in common. Both were undersized, victims of poor health while children and both were determined to build themselves physically. Both succeeded. Charles remembered vividly that Roosevelt boxed with his glasses on (a deadly risk, but without them he couldn't see his opponent's eyes, a vital part of boxing). Both were well read, highly motivated to learn about those subjects that held their interests.

CHAPTER 11

Lummis the Printer

At age twelve, Charles was presented with a small printing press, and several fonts of type, by his grandparents. It sparked an interest that stayed with Charles for life. Charles later said, "The wholly unexpected gift made me a printer for the rest of my life, incurable, though not always active."

In 1887, on his first summer vacation, Charles was hired as printer by the Profile House, a resort hotel at Franconia Notch, New Hampshire. His duties were to print up menus, programs and other announcements regarding hotel activities. He was unutterably impressed with the beauty of the area and especially of the spectacular wonder of the stone profile of the Old Man of Cannon Mountain, hanging over Profile Lake.

Charles had written poetry since the age of thirteen, with his father's encouragement. New Hampshire's rugged beauty inspired him to new heights. He spent every moment not on duty at the hotel, in a birchbark canoe exploring the natural wonders of Profile Lake and writing poetry in an effort to express his deep emotions. He even slept in the canoe so that he might miss nothing in a waking moment. Charles was familiar with birch trees and knew that their bark can be split into numerous thin sheets with paperlike qualities. He proceeded to write a book of poems and printed them on small sheets of split birch bark, two and seven eights inches by two and one eighth inches and bound them into a tiny volume he entitled *Birch Bark Poems*. Truly the Lummis genius at work! These he sold over the counter at the hotel for twenty-five cents. He also sent copies to his literary idols and received letters of thanks from Walt Whitman, Henry Longfellow, Charles Dudley Warner, James Russell Lowell,

Oliver Wendel Holmes, and best of all, his boyhood hero, Captain Mayne Reid, writer of boy's adventure books. In all he sold over 14,000 copies and largely put himself through Harvard with the proceeds. Now, very few of the miniature books are in existence and one would probably bring a small fortune at a book collector's auction.

These, then, were Charles' first literary effort, his first business venture, and as it turned out, a highly successful one.

Ten years later, in New Mexico, a copy of *Birch Bark Poems* stuffed in his shirt pocket would stop an assassin's shotgun pellet and quite possibly save his life.

During Charles' halcyon days at Harvard he seems to have suddenly stumbled onto the discovery that comes sooner or later to most young men. That is to say that his awareness of the charms of the "gentler sex" became acutely and swiftly awakened.

He was handsome, aggressive, exciting and excitable. It seemed as though the "gentler sex" was equally taken with him. Another product of his summer in New Hampshire, aside from poetry and printing, was a romantic alliance with a young lady named Emma Nourse. The issue of that alliance was a daughter named Bertha that Charles claimed not to know about until she was twenty-five and identified herself to him on one of his trips east.

On April 16, 1880 Charles married Dorothea Roads, a young medical student at Boston University. Her letters to him prior to their marriage leave little doubt that she was the pursuer in that romance. She was a remarkable young woman seeking a career as a physician at a time when female doctors were a rarity. Following their marriage, she continued her schooling (she had four more years of study to go). Charles continued his somewhat checkered course through Harvard.

It would be kind to say that his efforts were sporadic. He excelled at languages and classical history. He did well at natural history and was greatly excited by archaeology. Mathematics, however, was his downfall. He failed the examinations for trigonometry and analytical geometry which disqualified him to graduate with his class. Perhaps he could have made up the examinations with some tutoring. He evidently didn't try. He walked away from Harvard a week before graduation exercises, an action he regretted for the rest of his life.

The following spring Charles moved to Chillicothe, Ohio to manage his father-in-law's farm. Never having spent time on a farm, he plunged in, worked until he had mastered the task and promptly lost interest. He moved into town and became editor of the Scioto Gazette, a four page weekly newspaper. Here, it seemed, was the career he had been born for. His breezy writing style and his skill at reporting and observation won him an enthusiastic following of readers. He disliked the damp, humid climate at Chillicothe, however, and contracted malaria, as had many of the locals.

By the time Dorthea had completed her medical studies and joined Charles in July, 1884, he was ready to move on. He had been in contact with Colonel Harrison Otis, owner of the then weekly Los Angeles Times. Colonel Otis had offered Charles the post of city editor and a train ticket to Los Angeles, Charles accepted the job, but declined the ticket.

Chapter 12

The Trek

Instead, Charles determined to walk, following the newly laid Atlantic and Pacific Railroad tracks, the final link of rail connecting the East and the Southwest.

As a boy, Charles had been fascinated by Mayne Reid's Southwest adventure fiction. His interest in archeology, fed by visits to the prehistoric Indian mounds near Chillicothe had whetted his appetite for more. He learned that the Southwest contained many largely unexplored archeological treasures. These he determined to see at first hand. He made an arrangement with Colonel Otis of the Los Angeles *Times* and with the Chillicothe *Leader,* to send weekly stories of his adventures for which each newspaper would pay him $5.00. This provided him with a traveling income of $10.00 a week, which by 1884 standards was more than adequate.

This then, was the decision that launched Charles Lummis on a lifetime career of bringing the attention of the American public to the wonders of our country. It also launched Charles into the attention of millions, greatly expanding his self concept.

Charles was making a monumental wager. He was betting his physical prowess and self confidence against the unknown perils of a still not fully explored land. Although he did have a brief encounter with a wildcat in close quarters, his greatest danger would be from human predators.

Charles was at the peak of physical fitness when on September 13, 1884, he stepped off the train in Cincinatti and walked out of town, his destination Los Angeles, California. He was clad in almost skin tight knee length breeches, knee high stockings, a soft flannel shirt, duck coat and wide brimmed hat. His feet were clad in low topped button street shoes of excellent quality. They lasted until Dagget, California before they began to disintegrate. He wore a hunting knife at his belt and $300 in gold coins around his waist. In his pockets he carried writing materials, fishing tackle, tobacco, matches and a small revolver. His rifle and bedroll he had shipped to Western Kansas, planning to sleep in hotels until he reached the frontier. On his belt he wore a pedometer at every step of the journey. When he arrived in Los Angeles on February 1, 1885, he calculated that he had covered 3507 miles in 143 days of walking, a remarkable record in anyone's book.

Dorothea's reaction to this venture is not on record. Her opinions would have made small difference to Charles, once his mind was made up. She took the train and met him in Denver in October and then continued to Los Angeles to wait for him.

Leaving Denver in late October, Charles walked south, along the eastern face of the Rockies and into New Mexico. There, his New England prejudices received a jolt. In southern Colorado he had written of his first experiences with Hispanics (he had learned to call them "Greasers") as follows, *The Mexicans themselves are a snide-looking set, twice as dark as an Indian, with heavy lips and noses, long, straight black hair, sleepy eyes, and a general expression of ineffable laziness. Their language is a patois of Spanish and Mexican. These may be poor specimens along here. I hope so. Not even a coyote will touch a dead Greaser, the flesh is so seasoned with the red pepper they ram into their food in howling profusion."*

When he arrived in New Mexico, he found that in order to survive, he was going to have to depend on those "Greasers" for food and shelter. And, strangely enough, they took him in, shared what little they had with him and did all they could to make him comfortable. He began to learn their language and became fascinated with the culture; a fascination that would last a lifetime. He spent a week in Santa Fe although he was anxious to go on. There he met Don Amado Chaves, speaker of the House of Representatives of the Territory of New Mexico. A warm friendship developed between the two men and Don Amado invited Charles to visit his ranch and inspect ruins that had recently been discovered there. Thus began Charles' introduction to two cultures for which he would become a self appointed spokesman for life.

Chapter 13

City Editor—and Scout

While Charles soon became devoted to his position as city editor for the *Times,* the spell of the Southwest was upon him. When, in 1886, the Apaches, who had surrendered to General Crook, were incited to break out and fight again by a white trader who supplied them with whiskey at twenty dollars a gallon, General Otis ordered Charles to cover the campaign. Charles jumped at the chance.

As had happened to Gene Rhodes' father, General Crook was in trouble with eastern politicians for being honest with the Indians and for keeping his word to them. Those who spoke loudest against him stood to lose easy profits if peace caused the Army to be moved out of Arizona.

While Crook did not complain about the lies circulated by his detractors, Charles readily saw that there was a great need for someone to write the truth about "the old grey wolf at bay." Charles became that eloquent spokesman.

While he worked, he lived the life of the Army scout, became a skilled tracker, and took so great a part in the campaign that after he had returned to his desk, Captain (later General) Henry W. Lawton wired him to return as chief scout. Charles was willing but Colonel Otis was unwilling to let him go. Charles had been recognized as a top tracker even by Al Seiber, perhaps one of the greatest scouts ever to serve.

Having arrived in Los Angeles safely and at the absolute peak of physical condition, Charles seemed determined to set out to destroy the body he had worked so long to bring to perfection. Perhaps he deluded himself into believing that if he could bring his body to perform the monumental task of walking 3,500 miles, he could force it to do whatever else he wished of it. He began to smoke ten to fifteen cigars a day, consumed great quantities of whiskey, put in twelve hours at the office, came home, ate dinner, lay down on the couch for an hour and then continued working until the early hours of the morning. This regime he carried on daily for two years, insisting that he felt ready for anything after two or three hours of sleep per night.

His position as city editor did not require these hours of labor. They were voluntarily self imposed. He was more than carving a lifelong career for himself as a highly competent reporter and editor. He imposed these 21-23 hour workdays upon himself primarily for the attention it gave him. Colonel Otis, Dorothea, friends, all tried to get him to stop. The drive to prove himself superior was in full control.

Finally, inevitably, his body rebelled. Not however, until it had given him ample warning. He began to suffer numbness in his extremities. On December 5, 1887 he came home from work, ate his dinner and laid down on the couch for a short rest, as usual. To his utter surprise, he was unable to move, when he was ready to get up. His left side was paralyzed.

There has been a great deal of speculation over Charles' illness. Some have claimed it was a hysteric simulation of paralysis induced by exhaustion. Dorothea, who was busily establishing a practice as a physician in Los Angeles, diagnosed it as a stroke. Whatever the cause, Charles dragged himself to work the next day and had to be carried home by fellow workers. He went to bed for two months under Dorothea's care.

Dorothea and her care were beginning to pall on Charles. Perhaps his next move had been on his mind for some time. Perhaps not. He remembered that his friend of New Mexico days, Don Amado Chaves, had extended a permanent invitation to visit. He wrote to the Chaves family and they responded with a renewal of their invitation to return to the land of "the sunburnt mesas and ardent skies." On February 5, 1889, Charles boarded a train to New Mexico. His career as city editor of the Los Angeles *Times* was at an end. So, also, for all intents and purposes, was his marriage to Dorothea, although his dependence on her lasted a number of years, and Charles took outrageous advantage of her deep devotion to him.

Charles assumed that the Los Angeles *Times* would keep him on the payroll until he could recover. He was shocked to find out from Dorothea that *The Times* had dropped him from the staff after only three months absence.

Chapter 14

New Mexico Interlude 1

The Chaves family greeted Charles with typical Hispanic generosity, prepared to put this invalid to bed and see to his needs. Charles would have none of it! He rode the thirty miles from Grants, New Mexico to the Chaves ranch alone on a rented horse. Once there, he determined to be as independent as he could force himself to be, constantly testing his firm belief that "man is greater than anything that can happen to him." He became a skilled one-armed horseman and hunter, regularly supplying the Chaves table with game. Finally his concerned hosts permitted him to ride to outlying sheep camps with messages and food.

Recovery was slow, despite Charles' determination. Many days he was too ill even to make entries in his diary. At twenty-nine, he appeared to be permanently handicapped.

Meanwhile, Charles' relationship with Dorothea, whom he called "Dolly," continued to decline. Longing for each other when apart, they could not be together without emotionally devastating clashes. From the beginning, Charles had ruled their union with a bewildering ruthless and almost savage dominance interspersed with tenderness, kindness and charm. Later Dorothea was to write, "What monstrous joys and sorrows he caused those who were near." Turbesé, his daughter, once described Charles as follows: "My father had the deadly gift of the Byronnic lover. Tender, selfish, thoughtful, ruthless, broad, bigoted, the enemy of woman and her most ardent lover."

The letters Dorothea wrote to Charles in New Mexico were full of the ashes of a deep and selfless love trampled and burned. In April, 1888, she wrote, "It seems as if my heart had been bleeding for two years and then it stopped all at once and I haven't felt a thing, not love, or passion for many a long week. You have felt it, of course, and you can't be more surprised than I. However, your letter waked it up and if it's only to sting you, I can't help it and you must either forgive it or forget it and me."

Charles was deeply affected by Dorothea's letter. He immediately suffered another stroke and lay unconscious for ten days. Strangely, when he had recovered somewhat, he sent for Dorothea and she came without hesitation. The reunion was a disaster, as usual.

After Dorothea returned to Los Angeles, Charles wrote to her many letters full of love and longing. At the same time he was writing letters to two sisters with whom he had become acquainted at the hacienda of their parents, Don José and Doña Ysabel del Valle. The hacienda, called Camulos, was one of Charles' favorite retreats. Located in the Santa Clara Valley, its warmth and relaxed atmosphere, as well as the beauty of the del Valles' daughters, had drawn Charles like a magnet.

He returned to Los Angeles and Dorothea, but hadn't much more than unpacked before he was off to see the del Valles.

There he was greeted with the Latin ebullience and gaiety so alien to his own somber New England background, and which so delighted his lonely nature. He returned convinced that one of the comely del Valle sisters, Susana, was in love with him and he in love with her. He confessed all to Dorothea, who consented to a divorce.

It never entered Charles' head that the del Valle family's religion would not permit a daughter to marry a divorced man. When he found out it would take a year to obtain a divorce in California and swore he couldn't wait, Dorothea was there to console him. He turned to her for comfort when Susana did not reply to his letters, and finally, when the del Valles convinced him that while he was always welcome as a friend, marriage was out of the question, that what he had taken for true love was only flirtation, he was again reduced to a crushed small boy. And again, Dorothea took him in her arms and consoled him.

Charles returned to New Mexico to resume his fight with paralysis. He had acquired a new interest, photography. With his usual enthusiasm for a new adventure, he became a skilled photographer in a short time. In the 1880's, taking a picture involved lugging around a forty pound camera plus chemicals and five inch by eight inch glass plates. He immediately began to record the ancient ruins, magnificent scenery and New Mexican Indians of his time. His pictures were for the most part, masterpieces of composition. He dragged himself and his ponderous equipment into areas that had rarely been seen by the white man.

Perhaps his greatest photographic accomplishment, and certainly his most dangerous, was the pictures he took of the procession of the Penitentes, a highly secret and fanatic order whose participants whipped themselves with cacti and on a certain holy day, crucified one of their number. They called themselves the Hermandad de Luz, the Brotherhood of Light. In 1888 very little was known about this mysterious remnant of the Middle Ages. Los Penitentes discouraged observation of their rites, especially by Anglos, and cameras were strictly forbidden, but because the Chaves family after many efforts to dissuade Charles, finally agreed to help, he was able to get the first pictures ever taken of this barbaric event. While he photographed the procession, two armed men stood on either side of him for protection.

In the fall of 1888, Charles moved from the Chaves ranch to the Indian pueblo of Isleta, a few miles south of Albuquerque. He was not warmly received by the inhabitants, who cordially invited him to leave. This he would not do. Eventually the Indians accepted him and permitted him to stay. In time, they accepted him as a friend. They affectionately named him *Por Todos* because he always carried tobacco "for all."

In the end he won their undying allegiance by obtaining the release of forty Tigua children from Isleta who had been seized by government officials and dragged off to school by force. His stories published about the plight of the Indians and the brutal treatment they were receiving from government officials stirred much public attention.

Meanwhile, at Charles' request, Dorothea continued to write almost daily. When she felt he was strong enough, she reported that the Los Angeles *Times* had only granted him a three month leave with pay for half of that period. This meant that the *Times* had now severed him from their staff. This blow brought on a relapse and Charles seemed to have arrived at the end of his rope. He had no income, no money, no future, it seemed. He survived by writing articles about Pueblo life, and by selling his photographs.

In the fall of 1888, Charles became involved in New Mexican politics in support of his friends, the Chaveses, who were struggling to overthrow the peon system which had essentially enslaved thousands of native workers to wealthy landowners. In doing so he attracted the wrath of the head of a powerful clan and his life was threatened. A hired assassin was brought up across the Mexican border to silence this irritating little gringo.

On a clear midnight in February, 1889, as was his habit, Charles stepped to his door for a look at the stars and a breath of the crisp night air. He was met by a blast from a shotgun fired from the dark. Fortunately for Charles, the gun was old and worn and had been fired from far enough away that the shot pattern had spread by the time it reached him. One pellet nicked his little finger, one lodged in a copy of *Birch Bark Poems* Charles had stuffed in his shirt pocket. One passed through his cheek (he was yawning at the time), and lodged in the back of his throat, where it remained for the rest of his life. Two grazed his skull. He nearly died from loss of blood before the bleeding was stopped, but eleven days after the incident, Charles was writing again. The incident stirred up much public indignation which contributed greatly to the elimination of the peon slave system in New Mexico.

Eva Douglas

Among those who nursed Charles back to health was a beautiful girl from Lime Rock, Connecticut who had been hired to teach Indian children at the Catholic school at Isleta. Eva, who was also called Eve, was fascinated by this "famous" man. He was twelve years her senior, penniless and unemployed. He was married. He was also highly intelligent, persuasive and a warm, kind and romantic man when the need arose. Eva was intrigued by him and soon won over. They were married in March, 1891 and set up housekeeping in Charles' rooms at Isleta.

Sometimes they barely could provide themselves with their next meal, but they were too happy to notice.

On June 9, 1892 their first child was born. Charles intended to name her Dorothea, but the Indians of Isleta named her Turbe-sé, Rainbow of the Sun. The name stuck.

Charles had long dreamed of being a father. Some speculators suggest that his disenchantment with Dorothea was the result of a childless union. Charles saw himself as a storehouse of knowledge waiting to be passed on to his progeny. Turbesé was the first recipient of his ambitious dreams. It was not an easy burden for her.

Adolph Bandelier

In the days before Charles met Eva he had wandered, alone, over the New Mexico landscape searching out undiscovered wonders left by the ancients, to photograph. On one of these expeditions in August, 1888, a lone man wandered into camp in the midst of a blinding sandstorm and Charles met one of the most brilliant archeologists and scholars of ancient American cultures alive. He was Adolph Bandelier. He had just walked the sixty miles from Zuni but did not appear to be especially tired. The two men formed a bond of friendship that was to last until Bandelier's death in 1914. Together, they explored and photographed the mysteries of ancient New Mexico. Often they tramped over mesas and into canyons for weeks at a time with a few handfuls of chocolate, a bag of ground meal, the clothes on their backs and Charles' ponderous camera.

In 1892, Bandelier proposed that they go on an expedition to Peru and Bolivia to explore Incan ruins. He secured a promise of $7,500 from Henry Villard, builder of the Northern Pacific Railroad, to cover their expenses. Despite a reluctance to leave Eva and the baby, Charles secured them quarters in Los Angeles and he and Bandelier left for Peru in the fall of 1892. For two years they dug in ancient Incan ruins, digging out mummies covered with the dust of centuries and amassing a treasure of artifacts. By 1894 Villard's funds had dried up and Charles was home again, unemployed and with empty pockets.

For a time, he made ends meet by selling his photographs and stories of exploring the famous ruins of Peru, as well as the bulk of his Peruvian treasures to collectors.

In the years that followed Charles' return to Los Angeles, he became swept up into a number of crusades. He started and provided the name, The Landmark Club, for a group dedicated to saving Franciscan missions that had been abandoned by the church and allowed to fall into ruin. The foremost of these was San Juan Capistrano. Others included San Fernando Mission, and Pala Mission. Charles was never a Catholic, but he felt very deeply that these monuments of faith should be protected for future generations. The Landmark Club under Charles' guidance rallied to save the old Spanish Plaza when the Los Angeles city council voted to convert it into a public market. They even took on the job of straightening out the confusion of 280 duplicate street names. With his inborn energy and enthusiasm for whatever project held his attention, Charles rallied together enough support to restore these old missions that were in some cases nothing more than piles of rubble and rain melted adobe. That they are there for our viewing and wonder is the direct result of Charles' herculean efforts.

In 1902, Lummis, long a staunch supporter of the American Indian in his efforts to obtain first class citizenship -- against overpowering obstacles, organized the Sequoya League. Its motto, he said, was "To make better Indians by treating them better." In this effort, he had the solid support of his old friend, Theodore Roosevelt, by that time, President of the United States. With Roosevelt's help, Charles and the Sequoya League were able to aid some three hundred Mission Indians who were brutally dispossessed from their own land and forced onto a barren, nonproductive reservation by white real estate interests. With President Roosevelt's intervention they were able to override the Indian Bureau's decision to let the Indians fend for themselves in the desert, and to apply sufficient pressure to force the Indian Bureau to purchase land actually more arable than their original lands had been. In addition the Sequoya League worked long, diligently and without pay, to find markets for Indian basketry and weaving. Their most difficult task was to convince the Indians that they had no choice but to move to the new land.

Chapter 15

Land of Sunshine
At the Editor's desk again.

In 1893, Charles Dwight Willard, then secretary of the Los Angeles Chamber of Commerce, proposed to Charles that he take over the editorship of a small promotional magazine supported mostly by local real estate interests. It was called The Land of Sunshine, and was typical of the advertising efforts of businesses extolling the joys of life in Southern California.

Charles had no interest in advertising but he was stirred by the chance to become an editor again. He agreed to take the job provided he be given complete editorial control and the right to work where and when he chose. The salary was to be fifty dollars a month.

Typical of Charles when faced with a new project that offered a challenge, he immediately went to work to remove *Land of Sunshine* from its tourist brochure status. He changed the cover design, reduced the dimensions of the magazine to a size he felt was appropriate to his purposes. He then proceeded to convert the pamphlet into a full-fledged literary magazine.

By January 1894 his first issue was on the newsstands. Real estate ads were relegated to the back. Charles' views were clearly indicated by his first article, "The Seal of Spain--The Spanish American Face."

At the helm of *Land of Sunshine*, which he later renamed *Out West*, Charles' considerable talent as an editor began to make itself known. He gathered up a group of talented but relatively unknown young writers and artists and proceeded to give them freely of his time and editorial skills to help them polish their talents.

It was as editor of the *Land of Sunshine* that he came to the aid of the struggling young Eugene Manlove Rhodes. Charles was quick to encourage those in whom he intuitively saw talent. Charles' letters to Gene were always full of encouragement to do more, to do better! Gene badly needed this kind of criticism and help. Charles had a very small budget to back up his support. Standard pay for a story or a poem was ten dollars but it is likely that without the warm backing Charles offered, and his help freely given, Gene might have abandoned his writing efforts early on and the world would have been deprived of his brilliance and keen wit.

Gene Rhodes was by no means Charles' only protege. Others he helped include author Mary Austin, brilliant young artist Maynard Dixon, who provided much artwork for *Land of Sunshine* and later for *Out West*. He also published some of Jack London's early stories. After she became an established writer, Mary Austin later turned on Charles and proved herself unappreciative of the extensive help he had provided for her.

In every sense of the word, for over a decade, Lummis was the heart of the magazine. He used it to realize the goal he had expressed earlier to Adolph Bandelier of humanizing science and scholarship. To make science, archeology, geography, meaningful and full of life to all men, rather than the dusty dry property of scholars was a major goal. The magazine also allowed Charles a platform upon which to air his views on imperialism, the Indian problem, the Spanish history of California, the natural splendors of Southern California as compared to the East. The February, 1902 issue for example, contains a twelve page article on the history of the orange, a two-and-a-half page piece on the progress of the Sequoya League in its efforts to assist Mission Indians, a two page piece on the Landmarks Club, a ten page editorial (In the Lion's Den), all written by Charles. In his position as book reviewer, he pulled no punches in dealing with those he saw as having little or no talent, or who's views differed from his.

While Charles' prejudices often showed through his evaluations, he was a fearlessly sincere critic whose judgment was usually reliable. He was a stickler for accuracy of details, especially in books dealing with the West.

There seems little doubt that Charles' term of editorship of the *Land of Sunshine* and *Out West* represented the apex of his life as a man of letters. He set out to establish a genuine magazine of and about the Southwest that would measure up to eastern journalistic and intellectual standards. In accomplishing that goal, he created a vehicle that was a clear reflection of the man and his beloved country, the American Southwest.

In June of 1905, the Los Angeles Public Library Board, having determined that Los Angeles should have a male librarian, offered the job to Charles, who snapped it up like a hungry trout. In July, the *Out West* masthead carried the name of Charles Amador Moody as joint editor.

Moody had come out from Connecticut and joined the *Out West* staff purely as a result of having read *Out West*. In the ensuing year Charles' control of the magazine declined as he struggled with the problems associated with a growing library, often putting in fifteen hour days. His contributions to *Out West* finally dwindled to an occasional article. He had accomplished what he had set out to do with *Out West,* and as always, a new challenge demanded his full attention.

Following Charles' departure, the *Out West* went into a steady decline under several editors and its last monthly issue came off the presses in June, 1917.

Chapter 16

El Alisal
The Magnificent Dream

On November 15, 1894, a son was born to Charles and Eva. Charles named him Amado, after his close friend, Amado Chaves. He was a healthy blond child and the center of his father's world. Charles' dream of children to carry on the Lummis name was beginning to take shape. Central to that dream was a house he would build with his own hands, a house that would stand to shelter his progeny for centuries to come; a permanent legacy for his children and their children's children. It was a magnificent dream. The result was a magnificent house.

After months of searching, Charles found what he was looking for. He located two-and-a-half acres of land along the Arroyo Seco in what is today the Highland Park section of Los Angeles. In 1894 it was six miles from the center of Los Angeles, isolated and lonely, but it came with a wealth of building supplies in the form of rounded river rock for the picking up.

As usual, the Lummis family was almost penniless. Charles had always operated at poverty level but somehow it hadn't bothered him so much until now. He scraped up one hundred dollars to hold the property and began to pinch every penny that came his way. He became a tyrant over grocery bills until Eva wept when she brought them to him. That did not prevent him, however, from wining and dining all who came to his door in the old Spanish tradition of hospitality.

It took him three years to purchase the land and put up a four room shack his family could live in until the great house he was to build was complete enough to move into. There was a grove of sycamores on the land and Charles decided to build his house

Spanish style around a large patio or court in the center of which would stand the greatest of these, a mighty tree he named El Alcalde Mayor (the senior chief).

The property and the house were to be named El Alisal, a derivative of the Castillian word *aliso*, which actually means alder. It seems that Charles with his extensive knowledge of the Spanish language, would have recognized the error, but El Alisal was the name chosen, and El Alisal the name remains today. It is known that the word *aliso* had been used in connection with the land long before it was Charles'. There is still an Aliso Street adjoining El Alisal.

Charles started with a concrete floor, arguing that when it got dirty a hose could be brought in to facilitate cleaning. For fifteen years he labored on this stone structure, determined to build a house that would last for centuries. First finished was a large central room he called the museo. Into it went his collection of Indian baskets, pottery, and other relics he had not sold as well as paintings, and other memorabilia he had collected over the years. At one end was his library, bookshelves he had carefully made by hand. Dining room, kitchen, bath, living room, bedrooms, all came later. More bedrooms were added as the family grew. A bell tower, an attic and a cramped office Charles named The Lion's Den, comprised the second floor and were for Charles' exclusive use. Every ground floor room had a door that opened onto the large patio. In the south wall Charles placed a huge double door that opened into the living room. Each of this pair of doors weighed nearly a thousand pounds. The hinges were reproductions of ancient Peruvian ironworks. A large iron monogram designed by Maynard Dixon adorned this massive double door. After Amado, Charles' firstborn son, died on Christmas day, 1900, Charles closed the double door for the last time. It was never reopened while Charles lived.

Every window frame, every door, every timber that went into building El Alisal was hand formed and hung by Charles himself. He often said that "A man's house should be a part of himself. It should be enduring and fit to endure. Life and death will hallow it; it mellows the generations—if it outlasts them. It should be good architecture, honest construction, comfortable, convenient, ... something at least of the owner's individuality should inform it. Some activity of his head, heart and hands should make it really his." Charles also was often heard to say, "Any fool can write a book, and most of them do, but it takes brains to build a house." The result of Charles' efforts to provide his family with the home of his dreams, was magnificent and by no means the least of his accomplishments.

Presently, nearly a century after the house was begun, it stands in mute testimony to its builder's skills. Virtually unassailed by time, it is currently the headquarters for the Historical Society of Southern California.

Walking through the "museo" and on into the kitchen with its steeply tapered ceiling, one almost expects to see Charles perched on a windowseat, waiting to greet visitors.

Sadly, Charles' dream of providing shelter for his descendants was not to be realized. Sadder yet, Charles himself was largely responsible for the destruction of that dream, although he would never have accepted such a verdict.

In January of 1900, the year that his firstborn son, Amado, died of pneumonia, a second son was born, whom Charles named Jordan after his friend David Starr Jordan. The Pueblo Indians named the boy Quimu, Little White Lion, and Quimu he remained during his childhood at El Alisal.

On August 20, 1904, a third son was born to Charles and Eva. Charles named this one Keith, after California artist William Keith, whose works Charles greatly admired and who was a frequent visitor at El Alisal.

Now, with three children running about, brightening the grey stone walls of El Alisal with their laughter, realization of Charles' dreams of family happiness seemed secure. This illusion was not to last, however.

To assist him in getting his voluminous writings, and his extensive correspondence into print, Charles hired a succession of secretaries to do his typing and filing. Many of them were unable or unwilling to keep up with his 18-21 hour-per-day work schedule and demanding way, and dropped from sight. One of them eventually became his third wife. With others, Charles established romantic alliances.

The Lummis ego led Charles to record his extra-marital conquests in Spanish. The patient, long suffering Eva, who could read Spanish fluently, stumbled across one of these accounts, and this, added to years of being the recipient of Charles' self described bad disposition, his flare-ups of irritability, his name calling and cursing, finally forced her to file for a divorce and to move from El Alisal. When she left, in 1909, she took Turbesé, then sixteen, and Keith, aged four, with her in spite of all Charles could do to prevent it. Only nine year old Quimu stayed with Charles until he was old enough for college. Turbesé, his close companion during her baby years, chose to defend her mother against Charles. The "Lummis will" which Charles had seen in her as an infant came forth as a crushing blow to her father.

While the castle Charles had built with his hands would stand the test of time for years to come, the castles in his mind had begun to crumble and fade away.

The home he and Eva had scrimped and starved to build was now a nearly empty shell. Furthermore, while he had labored long and hard to make the Los Angeles Public Library into an institute of learning and research, enemies on the library board were working to get him ousted. He was too outspoken, he dressed too flamboyantly, his ideas were too unorthodox. He spent money recklessly. The staff loved him. He raised their pay, shortened their hours, had a lunchroom installed, and provided them with instruction in library procedures. He built up one of the best research departments in California and the Southwest to be found west of Chicago. By 1909 however, the opposition on the board had gained control and Charles was discharged. He was fifty years old, his health was failing, and he was once again without an income. He was also engaged in a brutal divorce battle with Eva's lawyers.

In letters he wrote to Bertha, his illegitimate daughter, at that time, he bitterly lashed out at Eva. The gentle woman to whom he had poured out his love seventeen years prior, when he had been forced to leave her to go to Peru, the one who had given him four lovely children, was now, in Charles' words, given to filthy personal habits, wildly extravagant, a poor housekeeper. In no way did he ever indicate that he might share some of the responsibility for the separation.

To friends who offered condolences over the loss of his family and his position as librarian, Charles insisted that he was delighted because he now had time to pursue other interests. In truth, he was as hurt as a man can be who has carried a dream in his heart for years, only to see it vanish when it seemed to be within his grasp. His physical health was failing, largely due to the excesses he had forced upon it. For years he had refused to accept his body's limitations. Heavy consumption of cigars and whiskey and lack of adequate rest were now taking their toll. The magnificent machine that had carried him all the way from Ohio was beginning to falter.

Chapter 17

The Southwest Museum

Charles' mind, however, was afire as usual. He took up the banner for the Southwest Society. As managing secretary he began again to work toward the accomplishment of another dream, the erection of a Southwest Museum. When, in 1911, a donation of fifty thousand dollars was made to the Society, he knew the museum was now attainable. Groundbreaking ceremonies commenced almost immediately.

Location for the site of the museum was the basis for some dissention among Society members. Multimillionaire Henry E. Huntington offered the Society a gift of property valued at two hundred thousand dollars, free of charge. Charles, however, had located a piece of property high on the brow of a hill overlooking Arroyo Seco (and El Alisal). The view of the Los Angeles basin was spectacular, but the price was forty thousand dollars. Charles convinced the Society that his site was more desirable. Mr. Huntington's offer was declined. Today, the view from the Museum Hill is usually reduced to one mile or less due to air pollution and access is rather difficult.

That year Charles was invited to lead an expedition from the School of American Research into the jungles of Guatemala, to wrest from the lush rain forest the magnificent Mayan ruins of Quirigua. He took Quimu, who alone seemed untouched by the jungle "breakbone fever" that affected the whole expedition. Charles remained well during the trip but within a month of his return to the states in May 1911, he began to go blind and in a few weeks had lost his sight entirely. Undaunted, he took Quimu as his "eyes" and in August, just a month after he had lost his sight, he went to New Mexico with the Southwest Society to assist in excavating and photographing ruins.

Again he shouldered his ponderous old camera, and with Quimu verbally describing what he saw on the groundglass viewer, and with no vision whatsoever of his own, continued to produce photographs that were for the most part, brilliantly composed. He made his way over the rough terrain by hanging onto Quimu's belt.

Upon his return to Los Angeles he personally directed plans for the new museum. Again without vision, but with Quimu's help, Charles began to draw up rough floor plans to scale, as he saw the finished structure in his mind's eye.

By late 1912, Charles' vision began to return. Although he complained that his eyes caused him much pain in the following years, and cataracts later threatened his sight, he never again suffered total blindness. As his vision improved he took more and more control of the building of the museum. His domination would eventually cost him dearly.

Charles saw the museum as his own, the child of his dream. He viewed it as the direct result of a lifetime of study of the Southwest and its environs. Through his own efforts he had made himself an unshakable authority on the geography, archeology and ethnology of his beloved Southwest. Though he carried no titles, he was always a central figure in the construction and content of the Southwest Museum.

Unfortunately, museums require large sums of money to function properly. Of this essential, Charles had none worth noting, but he was skilled in the art of awakening enthusiasm in the breasts of those who did. The money was forthcoming to build and operate the museum as a result of Charles' efforts, but those who were providing it felt that they should be allowed to take part in the planning and operation.

Charles' impatient, frequently abrasive insistence that things be done his way gradually turned those with a moneyed interest in the project against him. In 1915 he was finally convinced by friends on the board that it would be to the best interests of the museum if he would resign. Thus he was forced to abandon another great dream. Two years later he was forced out of the Southwest Society, the institution which he had used as a springboard to launch the Southwest Museum.

And so, the last great dream of a great dreamer was wrenched from his grasp. One by one, he had lost his library, his family, his museum.

In 1919, Hector Alliot, first curator of the Southwest Museum, and a beloved friend, died leaving a space that would be difficult to fill. Charles rather humbly offered to act as "fill in" curator until a replacement could be located. His offer was flatly refused. Even after four years, the museum board wanted no part of Charles.

The genius that had singlehandedly done more to embody the Southwest with a great spirit, with a being greater than the sum of its parts, with a cultural endowment that lifted it from the dust of distance to be, in Charles' own words, "The Right Hand of the Continent," was set aside, the brilliance of its light no longer wanted.

By 1923, old wounds had apparently healed and on March 1, Charles' sixty-fourth birthday, the Southwest Museum held a Founder's Day celebration. Old friends from all over the world sent greetings to Charles. Many subscribed to a fund set up to pay his taxes and mortgage. He was escorted to the Arizona room of the museum, and after speeches, a curtain at the entrance to the caracol tower was pulled aside to reveal a bronze tablet. Peering closely, his weakened eyes were able to make out the message, which read;

TO
CHARLES FLETCHER LUMMIS
IN HONOR OF HIS WORK
AS FOUNDER OF
THE SOUTHWEST MUSEUM
THE TRUSTEES DEDICATE
THIS TOWER NAMING IT
THE LUMMIS CARACOL TOWER

Charles was deeply affected by the display, but his hope was that the museum would put him back to work. Sadly, it never happened.

Chapter 18

"Always Your Friend"
Letters from Lummis

Jan. 21, 1918
Dear Rhodes:
Just got your letter of the 13th today. Have had the book (West is West) for several weeks; and by robbing my pillow have waded through it.

It is a Powerful Book. It deserved to have been printed by someone who knew a fount of type from a tin can, evacuated. It still hurts my Virgin Feelings to see misspelling and Typographical errors.

You have done a very extraordinary thing. Very uneven, in places hazy, not entirely pulled together to a final Draw-String Novel made up of episodes. But you have made the Best-Talking book that ever came out of the mouth of the West. The language they use on occasion is frequent and painful and free.

You have three heroes, any one of whom is good enough for a whole novel—and all so different that they would do for three. I think probably you were wasteful to chuck them all into one book. "Dick" and "Crooknose" and "Emil"—they are people. You also have some others.

And to my surprise you have some Desirable Ladies.

I surely hope that you will be shamed by this blacksmith imprint,and insist on a new edition, and go over it yourself, and not only kill the compositor and the proof-reader but also get yourself together a little.

You have gathered in a nice collection of misprints. But I was too interested in the book to proof-read it as I generally do. But I will remark that the horse on page one (1) is "Alazan", and with no "i" in him.

I don't know where the hell you got your "Penalosa" chapter but I haven't time to go into that now: that would be a "Nation Review."

So I am just chasing up what I can hit at a gallup,—

On page 109, you don't need any apostrophes for "two"s or "threes." And the mountain is Limitar.

Page 173, it is "enchiladas" and "atole" without the accent on the first syllable but on the second, where it is not needed.

I don't know anything about the three other books you mentioned—for I never read books any more. Life is too short. But I do know that you have written a wonderful book. And I wish you had taken more time to do it. And I hope you will take a little time to do it over again, and make it a new begetment. If you will do that, you will come near making an Immortal. And don't forget old MacGregor. He is a hero who is good enough—in fact, too damned good—for most of the whole novel. But as you have about four novels in one, I suppose I cannot fuss you. Only—get busy with it, and make it something that will live.

I often think back to the times when I first bumped your knuckles for doing just what you do now. I never saw any work of yours that I didn't admire. I never saw any of it that I didn't want to kick you for not doing it better, as you are perfectly competent to do. I guess I never saw any of it that I didn't tell you about it what I am telling you now—that you have done a great thing but ought to be ashamed for not doing it better.

"Caboza" is not only perfectly proper, but the only sane thing to say nowadays, likewise "palisada" A good many letters were interchangeable in the old Spanish—and for that matter, they didn't spell any better than the old English or the old French, both of whom raised hell with spelling as we know it now.

"Penalosa" has only one "s"—though in the ancient Spanish the "s" was often duplicated.

Of course "Xiqilpa" is impossible in Spanish. there must be a "u" after the "q". And you would do a great deal better to spell it with a "J" instead of an "X"—Jiquilpa. There is no such thing in Spanish as "Q" followed by any other letter without a "u" intervening. That is the way they make their "K".

As to any of your willfulness, I think I shall have nothing to say. I raise hell myself sometimes. But you ought to kill your compositor and proof-reader and bump your own head against the wall for seriously hampering a really noble book by your own carelessnesses as well as that of others. And you ought to get busy and make good on the whole thing. If the book has the vogue that it deserves, you can afford to get out a new edition with new plates. If you set out to do this, let me know plenty in advance, and I will certainly give you some advice about the "Penalosa" chapter.

All here is very tame and steady. We are taking care of the missions and preparing to seed the Southwest with little regional history-rooms to save their own mementoes, and the Southwest Museum is the livest thing you ever saw in education. And everyone is well and busy. And we have times here every now and then that would do your heart good and would even reconcile you to temporary absence from the East. If you could be wirelessed over here for one of our Sunday evenings, I think you would not mind the lost motion or Time at all.

Power to your elbow! I have enjoyed this book as few in many years. That is the reason I am fussing to cuss you about it.

With love and best wishes for you and yours,

    Always your friend,

        (Charles F. Lummis)

The botched job of composing and proof-reading *West is West* by the H.K. Fly Publishing Company is briefly discussed on page

64. A second edition was never accomplished. The book never received the recognition it so richly deserved.

The chapter entitled "Penalosa" addressed the arrogance and cruelty of the Spanish Inquisition and the Spanish conquerors of Mexico. Charles steadfastly denied that these were true traits of the Spanish heritage he so fervently espoused.

April 18, 1924
Dear Gene, Of Mine:

Booful letter, and I thank you. And I feel all right—but I shall feel very much better when I have some windfalls, and can throw something at you that might be handy even then. But I won't worry any more till it does happen so—for I take you in full faith.

I am greatly rejoiced at the word that you are getting well. It has been a corrosive in me right along to have you sick and in prison—for the best of the East is that to you or me. Now I hope and pray that things may come around for you to come back to god's country—which you and I can keep for our own, in despite of the million bellyaches of tenderfeet.

Glad you got my letter about your mother's funeral. It was sure hard for you that you couldn't come to her. And I am greatly distressed for you, too, over the fate of your sister. I know she will be better off—and surely you will be. For all of us are entitled to at most, reasonable Peace. You have a right to more than most, being gentle and generous. And even I have felt entitled to it—and have taken it. You would never know the old Alisal now—with the atmosphere of peace and comfort and helpfulness.

Charlie Russell and Nancy were here Tuesday night. He is a good deal better, and has discarded his cane. I don't know how they have done with the pictures this year—but he has some stunning new ones, and some marvelous bronzes.

Harry Knibbs is out at Palm Springs, writing. Turbesé is still

*in San Diego, but Frank is up in Hollywood on the Citizen. I am
holding out pretty well—there is too damned much to do , and I
am feeling it...*

*If there is anything that I pray for, it is that you may Come
Back—both to California and to your work. I miss you very much
from both.*

*With a great deal of love, as of many years, and with all good
wishes,*

Always Your Friend,
(Charles F. Lummis)

The letter written on April 18th is typical of many that
Charles wrote to Gene. It contains a warmth and affection that
could not be spurious. The concern he expresses is unquestion-
ably genuine. He had no time or energy to send false condolences
to those he did not love.

Gene's mother died suddenly following a stroke. Even had he
had the money to buy train fare back to California, it would have
been a futile and exhausting trip to accomplish little but atten-
dance at her funeral. His sister had died following a long illness
which had sorely drained his finances.

Dear Gene, of Mine:

*It is a long time since I have heard from you and Turbesé, who
has been with me for a happy three days on her way back from
Frank in San Francisco to her Lithrey Lair in San Diego has
heard nothing either—save indirectly through Mrs. Johnson,
who said her last advices from you are disasterous, disfiguring,
and disconcerting.*

*I am a pretty good philosopher about my own troubles, but in
spite of Virgil I will be darned if it is easy for me to stand the
afflictions of my friends. And I am not at all reconciled to having*

you sick nor in the East—which is a disease in itself. Isn't there some possible way for you to imitate the young Monk of Siberia— and break from your Cell with a hell of a yell—whether you do any eloping or not? To my trained medical mind, the only Balm in Gilead for you is to get West again. Selfishly, of course I want you here, but New Mexico would doubtless be quite as good for you as this debauched land of Flat-foots.

I don't want to lay any burdens on you of writing; but it would be mighty welcome to have a line from you and particularly with a note of hope in it for your coming.

Gertrude is dispensed, carrying a large subsidy, and is pursuing a Career at the U. of C. at Berkeley.

Myself, though still at skeleton scales, am much better than in a couple of years, my heart behaving better, the cat in my step all right, and my head working with reasonable fluency and considerable accuracy. I have had the Heinz varieties of hell in my help, and have been ripped up the back and down the front both ears twisted; but at present have a pair of Gold Dust Twins that are helping me bring Order out of Chaos, so that I hope very soon to have everything systematized in such fashion that the book work can go on. Incidently, we are shaping up for the Book of Verse (A Bronco Pegasus)—and I wish to the Lord you were here with your judicious Club to help me run them through the gauntlet.

Are you able to write anything? I hope so—not merely because we need everything you can write, but because the doing of it is the best mitigant for what ails any of us.

Let me have a line from you anyhow! And God bless you! With love and best wishes,
        Always Your Friend
            (Charles F. Lummis)

November 24, 1924
Eugene Manlove Rhodes
Apalachin, N.Y.
Dear 'Gene, of Mine:-

This is not a letter to tell you how anxious I am at not hearing from you and how apprehensive lest you are still suffering and bed-tied—though God knows I am wondering every day how you are and hoping that you may be mending.

I am holding out—stronger than I was, though my heart is always precarious, and my eye-sight matter for grave apprehension.

God bless you 'Gene—and if He wants to do me a special favor, He might turn your wayward feet to the trail which leads to Arroyo Seco!

With love and best wishes,
Always your friend,
(Charles F. Lummis)

June 29, 1925
Dear Gene, of mine:

It is a mighty long time since I have heard from you either straight or round the corner; and I am not advised as I ought to be whether you are well (or reasonably so) and what you are doing (if anything) nor nothing. I hope that things are reasonably well with you, and that you have strength to write the stuff that is so much needed and that no one else knows how to do. But I never see the magazine—it is all I can do to skim the headlines of the Times and I often neglect that for a week. Too much to do and very little strength (except in my will, which is tenacious and tough) and my sight so troublesome that I evade reading as much as possible, and it may be that I am missing whole broadsides of Good Stuff from you in some of the weeklies or monthlies.

Harry Knibbs was out to the Noise the other night, and we had a fine time. I am almost ready for the promised siege of Troy with him, where he is to come over and camp with me while we go over my poems, to see if he would include in the proposed book any that my modesty and good sense would lead me to throw away- or veto something which my own infatuations might lead me to include.

I have had a Hell of a year and a half on the clerical side; one very competent secretary for six months till she flew the coop with a beachcomber I had sheltered for a short time. Others of various sorts including some very good ones, but for a variety of reasons no stability—and a few who needed to be boiled in oil. At present on an even keel but putting my faith largely in a Minerva out of my own Jovial head- and fist. It took me about two months to make her, she is not quite dressed yet; but Miss Allwood is on her way to be a Model Secretary of the world—and she will never elope nor forget what I entrust to her. Sometime you shall have her photo. -6' tall 5' across the shoulders, with 15 drawers including 36 desk trays, and very much other storage space, wonderfully devised for Order and Classification. For the first time in ten years I shall have a place for everything—and I am slowly getting everything to its place. And the first fruits of this new systematizing will be the file of my poems duly sifted and arranged, and ready for Knibbs' kindly eye.

Quimu and his wife and ten months old Patricia are with me, and a great comfort. Turbesé has gone up to San Francisco for a brief vacation with Frank who is on the Chronicle. Habitually she is hermiting in a little shack in San Diego, where she can pull the door in after her and write - write - write.

I had a beautiful letter some months ago from Leonard Wood in the Philippines—quite away from the ordinary official had stirred up Memory, and he wrote me a truly human letter, wishing that he and I could live over those old days together.

This must have sunk into my subconsciousness; for some weeks later I found myself humming a line which couldn't be anything in the world but the refrain to a ballad. Never wrote one in my life but I am doing it now—about Geronimo, and have some 28 line verses already. Knibbs thinks they are Bully. We made him very happy at the Gamut Club, last meeting.

With love and all good wishes, and wishing to the Lord that I could see you.

> *Always Your Friend,*
> *(Charles Fletcher Lummis)*

General Leonard Wood and Charles had become friends while both were scouting for General Crook in the Apache uprising. When Charles couldn't return to his scouting at General Lawton's request, Wood took the assignment and ultimately assisted in the final capture of Geronimo. The two men remained lifelong friends. Wood later became governor general of the Philippines.

The ballad Charles refers to evolved into an epic poem named "Man Who Yawns", Geronimo's Apache name. The poem appeared in *A Bronco Pegasus,* published by Houghton Mifflin in 1928.

Chapter 19

The Sunset Years

In 1915, Charles married Gertrude Redit, one of the succession of secretaries with whom he had made Eva's life miserable. He still hoped for a house full of progeny. Gertrude, whom Charles called "Gre", had been scornful and patronizing of Eva while employed as a secretary, but could not abide another woman coming into the house in that capacity. Charles hired a young woman to help him rewrite an updated revision of his book, *Some Strange Corners of Our Country*, for Century Publishing Company. She had helped Charles' close friend David Starr Jordan to write his autobiography and soon became "Daughter-Heart" and the source of much friction between Charles and Gertrude. She worked tirelessly to help Charles, arranging his worktable and finding material that had been lost for years, much to Gertrude's disgust.

Charles and Gertrude separated in 1923. The secretary stayed on until May 7, 1924 when she packed up and disappeared while Charles was attending a Gamut Club meeting in his honor. With her went some of Charles' most treasured autographed letters and other valuables.

Now Charles was alone, ill and as usual, in financial straits. Quimu, who was working, could not longer provide the companionship Charles enjoyed so much. He became a rather pathetic figure, going about his daily shopping in the neighborhood markets, pulling a little wagon after him.

He managed, in 1923, to accomplish one minor dream. With the help of Arthur Farewell as harmonizer and Ed Borein as illustrator he produced a volume of fourteen Spanish songs, entitled *Spanish Songs of Old California*, in spite of failing eyes that were a constant source of pain. This volume, well received by the public, has recently been reprinted.

A revised version of *Some Strange Corners of Our Country*, to be called, *Mesa, Canon and Pueblo,* was the result of great effort by Charles, at the persistent urgings of Century Publishing Company, to provide some sort of financial legacy for his children. It was published in 1925. Later followed *Flowers of our Lost Romance,* published posthumously in 1929, and the last book he was able to complete, a volume of verse entitled *A Bronco Pegasus.*

In 1926, weak, stooped, looking twenty years older than his age, 67, Charles returned to New Mexico. The effect on his health and outlook was almost miraculous. He was invited to join the Museum of New Mexico in an archeological trek of some thousand miles and went without a second thought. He visited Gallup and became involved in the Gallup Indian Ceremonials. He counseled the Pueblo Indians, enabling them to resolve theretofore unsolvable differences between them and the government. He stayed a while with his old and dear friend, Don Amado Chaves, at the Chaves summer home on the Pecos River. There he fished for- and caught - his last trout.

He stayed for a short time with Gene and May Rhodes- and gave Gene a hard time about letting depression get the best of him. He spent time with John Collier, later Commissioner of Indian Affairs, and with another old friend who had in earlier years spent much time at El Alisal, Ernest Thompson Seton.

He went home much refreshed, to return the following summer. He traveled to Isleta, to renew old friendships among the Indians who had known him so well in his youth. He revisited the aged Sisters of Charity who had nursed him while he was paralysed. Even had Charles known how little time he had left, it seems certain he would have greatly treasured these times in New Mexico. They rejuvenated him, in mind, if not in body.

Perhaps he knew, with the acute perception of age, that his flight was drawing near its end. The stormy petrel wrote, in his journal, shortly before he returned home the second time:

"Over a month ago at home I had the impression that a spider or something bit me on the left cheek bone, 1/4 of an inch under the eye, and has kept a little bulbous swelling there ever since; not painful but not quite normal. In the last two days this feeling of distention has spread to the left half of my upper lip so that it is entirely numb. Think I will see Dr. Massie about it tomorrow".

When he returned to Los Angeles, Charles went to see an old friend and neighbor, Dr. Laubershimer, about his face. Charles later reported that, "the spider bite and paralyzed lip didn't interest him at all, but the right eye ... gave him 'grave' concern. Signs of a tumor...."

The medics spent much time studying the suspected tumor. Charles was distracted by the birth of a second grandchild, a daughter born to Jordan and his wife. Charles had hoped for a boy and had a name all picked out, Charles Jordan, but had concluded that, "we will not drown it in the other event."

She became Betty Jane Lummis, the second daughter of Jordan. Nonetheless, Charles beamed with pride.

In November came the bleak word. Charles wrote:

"Well, I have my ticket and destination—but not the train time as yet! I was never late for a train but once in my life—but I think perhaps I will miss a few on this road...I know a few more things I want to do at this end of the line than at the other...the verdict 'malignant'...said it was a bad case..."

October 5, 1927
Eugene Manlove Rhodes
Alamogordo, N.M.

Dear Gene and May:
  Yours of September 26, send to Isleta care of Antonio Abeita, was found here on our return today, and I make haste to answer.
  Glad you are safe in Alamogordo, and happy in the Old Home Town, and with a warmer climate and a lower altitude, with their beneficial effects on your respective gullets. I hope you will continue to flourish and grow strong.
  We had a wonderful two months in New Mexico, and topped off with the Petrified Forest and the Grand Canyon, getting home at 2:15 this afternoon and finding Quimu and Betty and little Pat—and also old Elena all well.
      Always Your Friend,
          (Charles Fletcher Lummis).

November 29, 1927
Eugene Manlove Rhodes, Esq.
Alamogordo, New Mexico

My dear Ingrowing Gene:
  I hope they haven't suspended you from any of the alamogordos thereabout but imagine there is little danger—Justice still walks in New Mexico with leaden heels. Would give six bits if I might crash your door and sit in with you-uns awhile—though I am not using much time in visitations nowadays, except a few minutes in the evenings with Turbesé, who is here just now, and means to be with me much as possible in the next few months.

My favorite indoor sport of Fooling the Doctors is still going on: but they have my number this time; so the fooling process relates only to a little stretching of the almanac. My little spider bite has blossomed out into an able bodied cancer, past remedy, but suseptible to some retarding and palliating, the specialists say. The ablest oral surgeon wanted to take out most of the bones in my mug, as a first step to making me one of those desiccated Ecuadorian heads; But Dr. Laubersheimer frowned on this emphatically and commended me to the Deep-Radio Therapy. Says I will live just as long, and be much more comfortable, and considerably prettier. Knowing my stubborn disposition he thinks I may be able to hold out for about eleven months yet--this generosity, being based on the fact that I fooled him twice when he gave me a week and a day respectively to survive. So I am taking the deep sea radio; and also they are salting my antrum with a radium mine of fabulous wealth—but they don't let me walk away with it, it is removed before I leave the clinic. But I am perfectly happy and resigned, I am glad I have had all I have had, and bound to do what I can in what elbow room is left.

Yesterday, while lying on the table for three hours, as I was unable to read, I managed to work out a missing verse of Geronimo which I hadn't been able to rope with many efforts. It is to fill the gap you pointed out, of giving a little Comparative Horizon. I enclose a copy and crave your sentiments about it—though of course, you don't know its relativity to the whole poem. This makes 29 stanzas I believe; and I think about two or three more will settle Geronimo's hash—just gap fillers in the sense, where I myself realize no break, but where the average reader would probably lose the trail.

I am trying to get Turbesé to camp here with me and be my Lithery Executor, also to help me meantime. I think if she were here I could get the autobiography at least into such shape that she could finish it properly. But she isn't strong, and has various other obligations, so I don't know yet. With Miss Carlova I can turn out considerable other stuff, but wouldn't venture to tackle that big proposition.

I trust you and May are feeling fine, and that your throats have reformed from their evil ways.

Thank the Lord I had the two good months in New Mexico-- not only for good memories but for a store of strength that will carry me several months longer than if I hadn't had it.

You remember Dwight Edwards, the fine baritone? He is dying of cancer fast. Miss Carlova and I were up there a few nights ago with the little guitar, and sang to him to his great pleasure. He is a fine fellow and very brave about it.

Turbesé and Quimu send best—so does Miss Carlova. The little family is flourishing grandly. With a great deal of love and all good wishes.

Always Your Friend,
(Charles F. Lummis)

Alamorgordo, N.M. December 6, 1927

Dear friend:

Sorrow and dismay at your tidings—surely or we were not human, we hug the thought of how many times the best of doctors have been mistaken, but if we take their opinions at par—even so, the sorrow is for ourselves. It is heads up with us and not drooping, when we think of you, gallant and gay on your brave new adventure, "running forward to meet the spring time." Why not? You have given to earth more than it gave you, your life has been "bold, fortunate and free", you have given earth and water to no man, you have much to be proud of, little to regret; you can say truly, (as I wrote to Knibbs on his feast night).

"Bristling with exploits, not with shoulder knots,
I, traversing the groups and chattering crowds,
Made truth ring boldly out like clash of spurs".

So, if the medical opinions have not happily blundered again,
I can say—and find courage to smile when I say it—"So long,
friend. Good luck: see you later".

May I keep the stanza of Geronimo? It was like you to write it
on the operating table—and it says forcibly what was very needful
to be remembered.

We are hoping that Turbesé "goes into camp" with you, and
that the biography marches; and we are happy for the memory or
your visit, dear Abdul. For ourselves, all goes well. We gained
strength rapidly here, with no setback. For myself I have not been
so happy in years—and my mountains are better than my memory
of them. As a by-product, the writing does well. If you see Dwight
Edwards, please give him my best wishes. And for you and yours,
my dear love.

(Gene Rhodes)

Dec. 10, 1927
Dear Gene, of Mine:

Your beautiful letter. But don't get "sorrow or dismay" on any
account of mine. Anything that Has to Be is All Right. I fight like
Hell against the Evitable—against the carelessness, the shallow-
ness, the selfishness, the meanness that we hit on every side. And
even Fate can't bluff me with a pair of deuces—namely, the
definition by fallible mortals that this IS Fate. I have met her and
tumbled her a good many times—as She Was Said. But I know
the Old Girl when I look Her in the eye. And it isn't a dirty eye,
either--I like her because she is the only Reliable Female. She is
the one that never changes her mind—in spite of the many
changes of her alleged by those not competent to touch the hem of

her undergarments. I love the doctors and never believe them. I love them still, but they happen to be right according to my own intelligence. But they are not accustomed to people so Perverse as I am in standing off the Inevitable. I think I can fool them again— maybe by a month or two—but that their appraisal is correct, there is no doubt.

Sure! Keep the stanza of Geronimo—and I'm glad you like it. Harry Knibbs gave me six hours of his good time the other day and night, and we went over the whole damned Ballad; and he sat up with it that night, and next day and advises amputation of three of my pet stanzas, including this, which he thought "apologetic", Also my own concluding stanza with Geronimo's own yawn, and to Hell with our Movie Life;

    (Yawn) give me back Geronimo
        the Line and Leonard Wood.

I have great regard for that boy's judgement; but a little also for my own. He knows better than I what the public wants now; I hope I know as well as he what the public ought To Get.

I am mighty glad that you and May are so happy and so much relieved in throat and so on, now that you are back in Alamogordo. I hope that Old Stamping Ground will continue to be good to you. Glad that the writing goes along with the renewed cheerfulness and freedom from bronchitis.

I fear that I will not see Dwight Edwards any more; for he is pretty far gone and I am selfishly occupied with troubles of my own—of which the cancer doesn't count at all, but trying to figure out the Order of Precedence in the things that may be done yet.

I hope for Turbesé back next week, and dearly hope that she will see her way to collaborate with me. But she is a hemisphere by herself, and I never try to bluff or coerce my own children. When they are little, they don't ask me "Why", but do what I say. When they are big, I don't say anything as to their procedure— except: "Can I help you"?

January 2, 1928

Dear Gene of Mine:
That picture of your Sierra Blanca is a corker! I imagine the photographer had a cheap lens and didn't know composition very well—but he has got a beautiful thing in a way that a better lens and a better artist might have trouble to duplicate. But to Hell with your Snow! I have gone through it deeper and harder than any of you—but I have had my share and will take no more in Mine—except in Photos, where it is entirely in place. And you are lucky to have that sort of a view out of your window.

Glad you realized that Harry Knibbs was wrong in wanting to cut off my last verse. He will be out tomorrow, for a final Donnybrook, on it. Since his fine and generous and long-suffering autopsy on it with me—and then by himself and with other surgeons, I have made a few minor changes—two or three of text, and two or three in location of verses—and now have a clean copy made. Of course he is rhetorically right in holding that: "The Apache was the last frontier—
the tragedy was <u>That</u>"
Is the actual climax. But what the Hell does the average American know or care about the Frontier or about the tragedy of its passing? A little less than nothing. You and Harry and I and Leonard Wood and a few old timers can understand that great historic and anthropological and sociologic truth; but you might as well talk Fourth Dimension to the infant class as to expect the average reader of Houghton Mifflin books or the Atlantic *or* Scribners *or* Century *to understand this as a climax at all.*

We had a wonderful Xmas; with all my four children here for the first time at all since July 1921. And I have seen Much Worse Brats! With the exception of Keith, the youngest, all have gentle memories of you, and wish to be remembered.

I am holding out very well, tho the Witchcraft Deep Xray sort of gives me the Evil Eye for a few days at a time, physically. But nothing phases my serene content, and I am happy as a pup with two tails.
>   *With all love and best wishes,*
>   *Always Your Friend,*
>   *(Charles F. Lummis)*

P.S. But Please don't water your ink or else get a new pen! I can't read any writing easily; and your last letter nearly pulled my eye out—and I don't know whether I got it straight yet—the letter.

May 8, 1928

Eugene Manlove Rhodes
Alamogordo
New Mexico

Dear Gene, O' Mine:
Delighted to have your joint letter of April 30, and to know that you are going to your old ranch on Sunday—Monday, anyhow!
I am glad to hear that you are writing gaily and with some efficiency on a half history of a half state, for half a century,—that is a pretty good Yob in itself. I am dead sure that you will Point with Pride, even if you didn't invent the tune. But I am particularly rejoiced that you can carry an empty gun anywhere, and wear shoulder straps, and otherwise adorn the Southwestern landscape.
Turbesé is up at Victorville, on a long, hard seige. She will have to be a good many months in bed; but she is happy and indomitable and fortunately has had such a thorough knockdown

that she is at last willing to Rest. Which she never understood the meaning of before. I hear from her every week, and she is very cheerful—of course.

Me, going gaily down the road, whistling on the way, six months on the Journey, this Wednesday, but holding out handsome. And since the last wrestle and Radium a week ago, I have been much freer from pain than at any time in months—haven't had to take any anodyne for nearly five days now...

Hope your bronchitis and bile and other trimmings are letting you alone—as of course I suppose they are in your beloved Alamogordo.

Bertha up in San Francisco, not at all well. Quimu and his Betty and their babies flourishing mightily.

I am getting quite a good deal done, all things considered.

With love and all good wishes,
Always Your Friend
(Charles F. Lummis)

Charles began to gather loose ends. Although he didn't know it, he had only a few months left. Though the pain in his head and his eyes could only have intensified, Charles gave little sign. Pain was never to be an excuse for lost labor. He became desperate to finish his book of verse, *A Bronco Pegasus*. He badly wanted help. He had asked Gene to help but Gene had declined, pleading that he was not enough of a poet to qualify for the task. He had recommended Henry Herbert Knibbs, a little recognized but highly talented writer of Western prose and poetry and a close friend of both Gene and Charles. Knibbs consented, and with his help, Charles finished on July 10, 1928. On August 13, Houghton Mifflin Publishing Company agreed to publish it. Charles was elated. Another dream had been accomplished.

As was indicated in his letters, Charles had been given a pain pill, anodyne, and now began a struggle to see how long he could go without its relief, or without the false comfort of whiskey. On July 10, he reported in his journal, "6 hrs. poems. 2 anodyne. 14 in 15 days". On July 14th, he wrote "14th, No drink...Just nach'ly don't touch a drop of Juisque all day. 1st time in many months or a year".

During his last time of blindness, Charles had learned to shave with a straight edged razor without seeing his reflection in a mirror. Now he took great pride in being able to shave himself without resorting to a mirror. On August 29th, he claimed his 5000th blind shave.

Charles shocked Bertha by making arrangements to have his remains cremated, but she and her husband agreed to see that his wishes would be honored.

On September 3rd, Charles made note in his journal that Henry Knibbs had written in his foreword to *A Bronco Pegasus,* "...In spite of Dr. Lummis' modest disclaimer, he is always a poet—in his living, his friendship, his environment. Had he lived in the days of Bertran de Born he would have been a fighting troubadour, serving impartially with song or blade, and a keen edge of each...fearlessness and sincerity burning high and clear throughout these songs of his adventuring."

By early November 1928, his last secretary, Helen Wilson, left. With *Flowers of our Lost Romance* yet unfinished, Charles was desperate. She returned, ill, on the 4th and promised to stay until the 15th. On the 5th of November he recorded the last entry in the journal but kept the diary going.

The entry for November 4th reads":...8 hrs. Romance. 0 anodyne. 2 in 65 days, 0, swear. 6 cigars, 55 min. guitar. She (Helen) goes 11PM, I work infinitely."

November 5th, Up at 12:15. Blind shower, shave. Fine letter from Amado Chaves.

On November 12, he made the last entry in his diary in a strong clear handwriting. It began, "Advance copy of Bronco Pegasus, 13 days late".

That night he hemorrhaged. The next day, when Turbesé arrived, he was in a coma. He remained comatose for a large part of the time, but would arouse to sing with Turbesé or to speak briefly to her and others in a clear strong voice, only to return to unconsciousness again.

On November 24, word was received by telegram that *Flowers of Our Lost Romance* had been accepted for publication.

And sometime on November 25, 1928, the stormy petrel that was Charles Fletcher Lummis, set his wings for the last time, and drifted away.

AT TWILIGHT

The fire that burned so high and strong
Has burned away at last;
And we are left, who loved so long,
The embers of the past.

And yet—We linger dumb and chill,
With thoughts the dead may know;
And shiver o'er the ashes still
That warmed us long ago!

Lummis, Charles Fletcher, *A Bronco Pegasus,*
Boston, Houghton Mifflin Company, 1928

On a wall in one of the rooms in El Alisal hangs a beautifully framed chart. It reads as follow:

CHARLES FLETCHER LUMMIS
(1859-1928)
Author, Editor, Historian, Poet, Librarian

Erected this building largely with his own hands

Wrote ten books on our Southwest & California

Founded the Southwest Museum

Created the slogan *See America First*

City editor, *Los Angeles Time* (1885-87)

Awakened Anglo-Americans to the value of Spanish American Culture

Awarded Knighthood by King of Spain for writings on Spain in America

Edited *Land of Sunshine* and *Out West* magazine (1895-1910)

Initiated preservation of California Missions

Founded Sequoyah League "To make better Indians by Treating them Better"

**Published Works of Charles Fletcher Lummis
in chronological order of publication.**

Birch Bark Poems, 1878

Pueblo Indian Folk Stories, 1891

A Tramp Across the Continent, 1892

Some Strange Corners of Our Country, 1892

The Spanish Pioneers, 1893

Land of Poco Tiempo, 1893

The Awakening of a Nation, 1896

The Gold Fish of Gran Chimu, 1911

My Friend Will, 1912

The Enchanted Burro, 1912

A New Mexico David, 1925

Spanish Songs of Old California, 1925

Mesa, Cañon and Pueblo, 1925

King of the Broncos, 1928

A Bronco Pegasus, 1928

Flowers of Our Lost Romance, 1929

Chapter 20

Wherein We Conclude

To reach back over most of a century and try to bring two Westerners to the attention of a busy world is at best a difficult task, especially if one feels as closely involved with the two as the author does. Such a closeness makes impartial judgements well nigh impossible.

At the rapid rate of social change in our world, the accomplishments of two men that occurred eighty or ninety years ago seems like ancient history to most. Yet these two men embodied much of what made our West great and feeds our general interest in the West. Most of the West as we perceive it, is myth, but the substance that begat the myth is sometimes more interesting than the myth.

Fredrick Jackson Turner in his book, *The Frontier in American History,* says "All that is buoyant and creative in American life would be lost if we gave up the respect for distinct personality and variety in genius and came to the dead level of common standards.."

In Turner's famous thesis (1893) he contended that the basic influence in shaping American character had been the existence of the American Frontier. The existence of the frontier had made Americans materialistic, aggressive, ambitious, wasteful, philanthropic, benevolent. Westerners, as a group, adhered to certain characteristics; personal courage, individualism, a sense of honor and justice, honesty, loyalty, the bond of a man's word, generosity, respect for womanhood, (if not for equality). All these qualities were to be found in our two Westerners, in varying degrees and according to their own interpretations.

Both men were small in stature. Both were approximately five feet, seven inches tall; and neither ever weighed more than 145 pounds. Both were well endowed with a small man's aggressiveness and determination to prove himself equal to or superior to others. Rhodes boasted of having had 65 fist fights during his lifetime. Lummis constantly reminded others of his ability to function long hours without adequate rest. Both demonstrated personal courage, individualism, generosity. To these and other Westerner characteristics they applied their own boundaries. Both men were fearless; both demonstrated valor in the face of misfortune, but Lummis was, himself, to blame for much of the tragedy that befell him, because, as Edwin R. Bingham, author of *Charles F. Lummis, Editor of the Southwest,* writes, "of his inability or refusal to exercise a less spectacular brand of courage, namely restraint." This was especially evident in his dealings with women. He seemed determined to make himself subject only to his own laws, and in the end he paid severe penalties for that determination.

Eugene Manlove Rhodes was absolutely fearless in his youth. Anyone who regularly mounts and breaks wild horses for a living, or who descends alone into hand dug wells to work in heavy rock dust and a constant threat of cave-ins possesses a rare kind of courage, but in later life Gene showed a shortage of another kind of courage, the unglamorous courage of self discipline and determination to reach a not immediately attainable goal. He too, suffered tragedy other than his chronic illnesses, that of self imposed poverty. He simply could not force himself to forgo any distraction or to sit at his desk and stay with a story until it was completed.

He was also cursed with a cowboy's overdeveloped sense of generosity which allowed relatives and others with sad stories to drain him of his finances when he had money to share and sometimes when he did not. Consequently in his last years he was constantly writing to his publishers, begging for advances on stories he hadn't yet written and he and May were deprived of much comfort and security in their declining years.

Neither Lummis nor Rhodes was ever able to accumulate any financial backlog. Of Charles, his daughter, Turbesé, once remarked that she didn't believe he ever possessed more than two thousand dollars at any time in his life. The man who could raise large amounts of money for very worthy causes appeared to be unconcerned about his own fiances, at least until he began to build El Alisal.

Both men were individualists: Charles worked hard at it. Both men possessed a high regard for honor and justice. Both were honest to a fault although Gene was known to have fractured the law considerable in his younger days, and Charles was known to be rather creative with the facts in his early writings.

Both men were immensely loyal, both to their friends and to the various causes they supported and fought for. Either would fight to the bitter end to help a friend in the face of damning evidence against him. Gene defended and supported Senator Fall to the end of his life despite the part Fall was alleged to have played in the Teapot Dome scandal.

Both men valued friendship highly. Both men were, as a rule, extremely kind, sincere and warm to those who approached them. Both men were hospitable to a degree that frequently caused consternation to their wives, especially when they showed up with unannounced guests for dinner, as they were both prone to do. Gene did this much less frequently than Charles, simply because he and May hadn't the money to entertain. Charles thrived on regular gatherings of friends at El Alisal, whether he could afford them or not. Frequently he couldn't. Lavish meals followed by singing or other entertainment, attended by Charles' writer and artist friends, occurred regularly.

It is rumored that on more than one occasion those friends surreptitiously passed the hat to defray Charles' expenses. It is also evident that Charles used those hospitable times to place himself in the center of attention. Nonetheless, invitations to those "noises" as Charles called them, are rarely turned down and many wanted to be invited who never were.

In an age when letter writing, especially among well educated people, was considered the ONLY way to communicate, both Gene and Charles were highly skilled at expressing themselves with the written word. And they wrote so many letters that one wonders how they got anything else done.

Charles' letters, and Gene's, for that matter, consistently demonstrated a graciousness and warmth that would have been difficult to falsify. Charles, in his role as editor, however, never hesitated to play the Dutch uncle, or to scold in his correspondence with Gene Rhodes or Mary Austin or Maynard Dixon if he felt it needed. Professionally, he had no patience with mediocrity. He would brook no excuses. He would accept no writing or artwork he felt was not up to the artist's capabilities. He took Gene to task for letting himself succumb to depression during a lengthy illness. He verbally trounced Mary Austin for what he considered flagrant misuse of Spanish terms and, in essence, accused her of sloppy writing. When Maynard Dixon wrote that he had been unable to paint because of marital problems, Charles offered no sympathy but declared that hard work was the only cure for such ills. But in his letters to each of these, his protegés, the blows were softened by expressions of affection and genuine concern that eased the sting.

Pasó Por Aquí!

And so, these two men, giants with clay feet, passed by here: The one a master of literature, the other a master at bringing to the public's view the wonder of Southwestern history, archeology and ethnology, as well as a master champion for the American Indian and the Hispanic culture of Southern California.

Today, not yet a century since they passed this way, they are largely forgotten. Nothing much tangible remains to indicate Gene's route but a collection of letters that are almost impossible to read, and the few books he wrote, which are for the most part tightly clutched by a small but intense group of fans and collectors. A large rough stone marks his final resting place. Perhaps the best evidence of his passing, and his greatness, is the late W. H. Hutchinson's biography, *A Bar Cross Man*.

There are far more tangible reminders of Charles' passage; but in spite of the physical evidence of the magnificent Southwest Museum and the rock pile known as El Alisal, which literally thousands of people pass daily on the Pasadena Freeway, you might question natives of Los Angeles and southern California all day and not find one who has ever heard of Charles Fletcher Lummis. Those few you might find who know the name seldom know—or understand—or care about—what he stood for.

Eugene Manlove Rhodes was essentially a range man whose emotional makeup clashed with his profession like a square peg in a round hole. He was constantly at odds with himself. If it had not been for May's unstinting support, it is unlikely that he would ever have completed more than a few short stories and poems in his lifetime. His intelligence, wit and graciousness were like highly polished facets on an otherwise rough stone.

Charles Fletcher Lummis was a man of such complexities that it is surprising that more people have not tried to analyze his behavior. A trained psychologist could have a field day with the influence of being raised without a caring mother and its ultimate effect on his perception of women. Egocentric to such a degree that his personal stationery carried a picture of him on every page, his self destructive tendencies brought him misery, pain and paralysis. He was arrogant, ruthless, domineering, selfish. He was also gutsy, whimsical, compassionate (to those whose causes he supported), a visionary of rare brilliance, who remained blind to his own faults. To his children he gave unstinting love but little understanding. To his friends he gave himself. He rarely hated his enemies, who were legion.

The following is partly pure Gene Rhodes and partly the author's. It is the author's opinion that it should be deeply carved on both these men's gravestones.

EPITAPH FOR A GOOD MAN ...
HE KEPT HIS PROMISES,
HE FINISHED WHAT HE STARTED,
—AND HE PAID FOR WHAT HE BROKE.

No man could ask for a better one.

A TRIBUTE TO KEITH LUMMIS

Keith Lummis (called Hluru, Little Rain, by his father's Indian friends of Isleta Pueblo in New Mexico) was named after his godfather, William Keith, a highly talented artist and a close friend of Keith's father. Keith was born on August 20, 1904 in his father's home, El Alisal, in Los Angeles. When his mother, Eva Douglas Lummis, divorced Charles in 1909, Keith, his sister, Turbesé, and his mother left El Alisal and Keith did not return until he was eighteen.

Keith attended schools in southern California, finishing his high school years in a military academy. At eighteen he went to sea as an ordinary seaman on a merchant vessel. At nineteen he enrolled at the Univerity of Arizona at Tucson where he joined the Reserve Officer's Training School. Already a skilled horseman, he served a time with the famed black 10th Cavalry at Fort Huachuca, Arizona. In 1927, he joined the United States Border Patrol. He was appointed to serve as an agent of the Internal Revenue Service in 1930, enforcing the Prohibition Act. In 1943, he became one of 250 agents of the United States Secret Service.

During the decade following World War II, Keith served in the United States Foreign Service, but later turned his back on government service to become manager of a ski lodge in the Sierras, primarily because he was an avid skier and saw an opportunity to pursue his interest and at the same time provide a home for his children.

Keith, now 89, shares a comfortable home with an unsurpassed view of the Pacific Ocean, with his gracious wife, Hazel, and with fond memories of four beautiful children, now grown and with families of their own. They appear often in Keith's conversations, as well they should.

In one lifetime, Keith Lummis has crowded more living, and more joy of living, more exciting and occasionally more dangerous experiences than most men dream of.

At 89, the eyes are dimming and the joints occasionally rebel, but Keith's mind is as young as tomorrow. Still straight and tall, he uses a came as a flying buttress to shore up limbs no longer completely dependable. As befits a Lummis, for whom adventure is the stuff of life, the unassuming cane conceals a blade of Toledo steel.

No television dominates the Lummis living room. Ideas, books, art and the rich tapestry of Keith's past, his travels abroad, his many literary and scholarly contacts, his wide knowledge of the world and his interest in the history of the American Southwest serve to keep him busy. His sense of humor and his refusal to take himself too seriously make any personal contact with him a pleasurable and a comfortable experience.

Keith is a skilled historian of the American Southwest, an avid reader, when his failing eyes permit, and an accomplished photographer, as was his father, Charles.

Most of all, Keith is a gentleman in the truest, simplest defintion of the word: i.e., a man who knows he is a man and can therefore afford to be gentle with all others because he has nothing to prove.

Eugene Manlove Rhodes once implied that the mark of a good man was that he: Keeps his promises,
Finishes what he starts, and
Pays for what he broke.

All of which applies, in spades, to hizzonor, Keith Lummis.

—*Frank Clark, 1993*

BIBLIOGRAPHY

Austin, Mary. *Earth Horizons:* Autobiography. Boston, 1927.

Bandelier, Adolph. *The Delight Makers.* New York, 1916.

Bingham, Edwin R. *Editor of the Southwest.* San Marino, California, 1955.

Fiske, Turbesé Lummis and Lummis, Keith. *Charles F. Lummis, The Man and His West.* Norman, 1975.

Gordon, Dudley, *Crusader in Corduroy.* Los Angeles, 1972.

Hutchinson, W.H. *A Bar Cross Man.* Norman, 1956.

Rhodes, May, D. *The Hired Man on Horseback.* Boston, 1938.

INDEX

Apache Indians, 99
Apalachin, New York, 49
Atlantic and Pacific Railroad, 96
Austin, Mary, 110, 147
Ballad of Geronimo,134, 137, 138
Bailey, May, 130
Bandelier, Adolph Franz, 107
Bar Cross Edition of Works of Eugene Manlove Rhodes, 81
Beyond the Desert, 81
Belle Acres, 84
Billy the Kid, 22
Birch Bark Poems, 93, 105
Boer War, 20
Borien, Edward, 81
Brave Adventure, The, 52
Bronco Pegasus, A, 52, 76, 77, 129, 140, 142
Brothers of Light: see Penitentes
Burns, Walter Noble, 65

Calvin, Ross, 82, 83
Carey, Harry and Olive, 58, 59, 61
Catron, Thomas, 33, 34
Chaves, Amado, 98, 100, 112, 131
Chilicothe, Ohio, 95, 96
Comfort, Will Levington, 57
Costain, Thomas, 81, 82
Crook, Gen. George, 99

Davison, Emma Antoinette, 32
Davison, Mr. and Mrs. Lucius, 50, 62, 125
DeVoto, Bernard, 27, 28
Dixon, Maynard, 110, 113, 147

El Alisal: building of, life at, guest at, later use, 112, 113, 114, 148
El Paso, Texas, 20
Engle, New Mexico, 17

Fall, Albert Bacon, 64, 146
Fiske, Frank, 60, 125
Fiske, Turbesé Lummis, 59, 60, 61, 102, 106, 139
Flowers of Our Lost Romance, 131, 142
Fly, H. K., 66, 123
Ford, John, 59
Forsha, Fred, 33
Fort Stanton, 16, 31
Franconia Notch (New Hampshire), 93

Good Man and True, 83, 84
Grey, Zane, 25, 27

Hatchet Cattle Company, 64
Henderson, Alice Corbin, 63
Historical Society of Southern California, 114
Hired Man on Horseback, The, 62, 82,
Hough, Emerson, 53
Houghton Mifflin Publishing Company, 27, 129, 138, 140
Huntington, Henry, 117
Hutchinson, W. H., 7, 44, 55, 59, 85, 148

Indians, Aid to, 108
Isleta, New Mexico, 104, 105, 106, 131

Jordan, David Starr, 114, 130

Knibbs, Henry Herbert, 124, 128, 137, 138, 140, 141

Land of Sunshine, 25, 38, 109, 110, 111
Landmarks Club, 107, 108
Lincoln, New Mexico, 13, 22, 23
Lion's Den, 113
London, Jack, 110
Los Angeles, 56, 57, 58
"Loved I Not Honor More", 20, 21,
Lummis, Amado, 112
Lummis, Bertha, 94, 116, 140, 141
Lummis, Dorothea Rhoads, 94, 95, 102, 103, 105
Lummis, Gertrude Redit, 130
Lummis, Jordan, 114, 115, 117, 118, 130, 132, 133, 135, 140
Lummis, Keith, 8, 114

McSween, Susan, 64, 77
Marmion Way, Los Angeles, 55
Martin, Robert, 30, 33
Mencken, H. L., 28, 29
Mesa, Canon and Pueblo, 131
Mescalero Reservation, 19, 31
Missions, 107, 108

New Mexico, 13, 14
Old Timer's Book, 81

Otis, Colonel Harrison Gray, 87, 88
Out West, 110, 111
"Over, Under, Around and Through", 49

Pacific Beach, California, 64, 80
Pasadena, California, 31
"Penalosa", 122, 124
Penitentes, 104
Phillips, Henry Wallace, 53
Purple, Fred, 32,50
Purple, Jack, 43, 50

Quimu, see Lummis, Jordan

Reid, Capt. Mayne, 94, 96
Rhodes, Alan, 44, 50
Rhodes, Col. Hinman, 17, 31
Rhodes, Barbara, 50, 51, 52
Rhodes, Clarence Edgar, 31
Rhodes, Helen Mabel, 31, 125
Rhodes, Julia Manlove, 24, 31, 32, 55
Rhodes, May Louise, 30, 32, 42, 43, 44, 45, 72, 85
Rhodes' Pass, 17
Rogers, Will, 57
Roosevelt, Pres. Theodore, 91, 92
Russell, Charles M., 124

San Andres Mountains, 84
San Diego, California, 64, 80
"Sandy Shuffleshorn", 61

Santa Fe, New Mexico, 63, 74
Saturday Evening Post, 54, 62, 65, 81, 82
Schultz, James Willard, 57
"See America First", 88
Seltzer, Charles Alden, 27
Sequoya League, 108
Sisters of Charity, 131
Southwest, 88, 99, 116
Southwest Museum, 117, 118, 119, 129
Spanish Songs of Old California, 130

Three Rivers, New Mexico, 64
Tigua Indians, 105
Tularosa, New Mexico, 43

Wallace, Lew, 16
Webb, Walter Prescott, 27

About the author

Frank M. Clark was born in a converted boxcar during the oil boom in Burkburnette, Texas in 1924. He grew up on the Kansas-Oklahoma border, not far from where the Santa Fe trail crossed the Arkansas River and where Coronado wandered in search of Quivira.

The Southwest was an important part of his childhood. His grandfather was a peace officer in charge of the Oklahoma division of the Santa Fe Railroad, who knew personally, famous western lawman Bill Tilghman and who was instrumental in the capture of Jeff Spurlock, New Mexican bank and train robber in 1916.

Clark finished high school in 1943 and after two years working on the Santa Fe Railroad, migrated west. For the next several years he was a dishwasher, fry cook, book store clerk, warehouseman, ranch hand, truck driver's helper, library assistant, movie house projectionist. He worked in a number of towns including Hood River, Oregon, Albuquerque, New Mexico, and Colorado Springs, Colorado.

Following twenty one years of teaching in the California public schools, Clark retired in 1980 and moved to Tehama, California on the Sacramento River. Always an avid western historian, he occasionally teaches a class on the History of the American Frontier for the Shasta Community College in Redding, California.

While managing a bookstore in Chico, California, in 1948, Clark had the good fortune to make the acquaintance of author W. H. Hutchinson, who greatly influenced, aided and abetted his research for *SANDPAPERS* until Hutchinson's death in 1990.

Send for our free catalog

and find out more about our books on:

- ❖ The Old West
- ❖ American Indian subjects
- ❖ Western Fiction
- ❖ Architecture
- ❖ Hispanic interest subjects
- ❖ And our line of full-color notecards

Just mail this card or call us on our toll-free number below

_____

Name

_____

Address

_____

City   State   Zip

Send Book Catalog _____ Send Notecard Catalog _____

Sunstone Press / P.O.Box 2321 / Santa Fe, NM 87504
(505) 988-4418   FAX (505) 988-1025   (800)-243-5644